Praise for *The Best Job in the World*

Vic Goddard speaks from the heart but never fails to use his head. The man who defended his school against the tabloid press now tackles those who snipe at headship without understanding its value, its pressures or its rewards. Teachers need to be leaders. Vic shows them how.

Gerard Kelly, former editor, *TES*

Working with Vic is a rollercoaster, but one where the designer has missed out the downward bits but has managed to keep in the loops. Vic describes the Passmores' experience and his centrality to it perfectly. This book captures beautifully how Vic Goddard's school works. It is a special community to be part of and I was privileged to play my part.

Stephen Drew, head teacher, Brentwood County High School (former deputy head teacher at Passmores Academy)

Chronicling his time as a teacher and head teacher, Vic's book gives us a unique insight into his career, the decisions he's made (good and bad) along the way and the reasons behind his ideas and methodology.

Vic's absolute love for his job is driven by his belief that every child matters and that the impact education has on that child can be life changing.

Tactics on how best to run a school, acknowledging one's strengths and weaknesses, improving your leadership ... this book is a practical guide packed full of personal wisdom.

Not only recommended for the teaching profession, but an inspiring read for anyone interested in making the most of their potential.

We can all learn something from Vic Goddard.

David Clews, head of documentaries, TwoFour

Any teacher wavering over whether or not to take the next step to becoming a school leader will get a confidence boost from Vic Goddard.

As well as providing insight into the school that was the stage for *Educating Essex*, Vic makes an entertaining case for head teachers to model themselves on a rather different TV success: the celebrity chef Gordon Ramsay (though, hopefully, without quite as much swearing).

Michael Shaw, *TES*

What I love about *The Best Job in the World* is its readability. Its narrative pings along at a pace and Vic's story of his life as a head teacher is compelling. But it's much more than a reality TV star's tale – it's about what it's like to be a head teacher in England right now and how head teachers like Vic are holding on to their moral purpose amidst tumultuous educational change. It's a rollicking good read; as an insight into headship I reckon it's unrivalled.

John Tomsett, head teacher, Huntington School, York

I loved this book. It is a frank, jargon-free and humane account of headship. Above all, Vic reminds us that schools are so much more than the last exam results or Ofsted grade. They are infinitely complex places, led by real human beings who carry the weight of everyone else's expectations. The best job in the world maybe but read this book and be grateful to those who do it.

Fiona Millar, *Guardian* Education columnist

THE BEST JOB
IN THE WORLD

VIC GODDARD

Independent Thinking Press

First published by

Independent Thinking Press
Crown Buildings, Bancyfelin, Carmarthen, Wales, SA33 5ND, UK
www.independentthinkingpress.com

Independent Thinking Press is an imprint of Crown House Publishing Ltd.

© Vic Goddard 2014

The right of Vic Goddard to be identified as the author of this work has been asserted by him in accordance with the Copyright, Designs and Patents Act 1988.

First published 2014.

British Library Cataloguing-in-Publication Data
A catalogue entry for this book is available from the British Library.

Print ISBN 978-1-78135-110-9
Mobi ISBN 978-1-78135-160-4
ePub ISBN 978-1-78135-161-1
ePDF ISBN 978-178135-162-8

Edited by Fiona Spencer Thomas

Author photograph © Susannah Ireland

Printed and bound in the UK by
TJ International, Padstow, Cornwall

Family comes in many forms

Dad, I wish you had been around to see the last couple
of crazy years – I hope you would be proud

Contents

Foreword by Ian Gilbert .... *i*

Acknowledgements .... *v*

Introduction 1

Part one

1   If I Can Do It, Anyone Can 7

2   Twitter Chatter 17

3   The Great TV Experiment 21

4   The Aftermath 37

5   'I Don't Want to be a Head Teacher' 49

6   It's a Lonely Life, or Is It? 61

7   Self-Doubt 65

8   Change for Change's Sake? 71

9   From Government to Governors 75

10   The Five P's of Successful Leadership 79

11   The Path to Headship 103

Part two

12   The Gordon Ramsay-Style School Improvement
     Model 111

13   The Menu, or Curriculum 115

14   Sacking the Head Chef, or Getting the Right People
     On the Bus Before Deciding Who's Driving 121

15   Asking the Customers, or How Do We Provide for the
     Community? 129

16   Painting It White, or Giving the Students the
     Environment They Deserve 135

17   Our Ethos 143

18   Our Vision at Passmores 151

Foreword

In Chile, pushing a man dressed as a panda playing the guitar into a swimming pool is peak-time TV viewing. As a result of this, I didn't get to watch a lot of telly in 2011 when I was living in Santiago. However, via the magic of Twitter, I kept catching a great deal of excitement about a programme called *Educating Essex* and the name 'Vic Goddard' kept cropping up.

From what I could make out from the tweets, there seemed to be a lot of viewers crying a lot of the time.

A year later, I found myself face to face with Vic in his office at Passmores and I was probably about the only person in the country who didn't already feel like they knew him and the school personally and professionally. That soon changed.

What came across was a man who was as disarmingly honest and unpretentious in his approach to school leadership as he was hyperactive. Since that first meeting, I've had the pleasure of seeing Vic in action at school, of witnessing his ability to interact seemingly effortlessly with staff, students and parents, in meetings with senior politicians, delivering keynote conference addresses and interacting with other Independent Thinking Associates. What comes across on all these occasions comes across in this book: 'This is me. This is how I see it. Take it or leave it. But never doubt that I am ever anything less than one hundred per cent in it for the children.'

I immediately wanted him to write a book for Independent Thinking Press, not because he's been on the telly – who hasn't these days? – but because he is an infectiously remarkable head teacher.

Fast-forward a year and I'm standing outside the impressive entrance to Passmores, briefing a delegation of Chilean teachers from an educational charity I am supporting through my company, Independent Thinking, on how to greet people in England. In Chile, shaking hands, kissing on the cheeks and hugging is how you greet your bank manager, let alone your friends and family. I felt I had to warn the young Chilean teachers that we didn't indulge in such practices in England and that a polite handshake was about as much physical contact as we could tolerate with strangers. Two minutes later, we walked into reception to be met by Vic, who gave me a huge bear hug and the Chilean delegation were won over from the start.

What most impressed them, apart from seeing a well-run school where the needs of all children, from the most vulnerable to the most able, were catered for to an extraordinarily high level, was the way in which Vic was able to communicate with such ease and good humour with all members of the school community, while still managing to retain the authority and respect of everyone in the school. Rather than acting 'like a head teacher' Vic was himself and that worked.

At one point during our visit, he needed to address the whole school on the matter of a graffiti incident that had occurred that week, a rare problem for the school. All staff and students were gathered in the 'heart space', as it is known, the central open space that serves as a community area, break-out space and dining room at the heart of the school. From one of the balconies looking down on it, surrounded by the senior students, Vic spoke calmly about what had happened and how it would stop. No threats. No emotional guilt trips. No 'I want names!' rants. Just telling it how it is. Below him and around him several hundred students and staff stood perfectly still and in silence, listening to every word. It was a remarkably intimate and mesmerising school address, far more powerful than trooping children in rows into a school assembly hall to be lectured at and threatened as I have seen on so many occasions elsewhere. The whole event finished with a minute's silence and a bugler from the Salvation Army playing the 'Last Post', which Vic assured me was because it was Armistice Day and that he didn't always have a trumpeter when he spoke.

One of the things he made clear to his students over the graffiti incident was that it was important for them not to be part of the problem but to be part of the solution. There was an issue and it was up to each of them, as members of the school community, to work out what they were going to do about it.

In many ways, this book has the same message.

If you feel there is a problem with education today, if schools are not what you would want them to be, if you think we are heading off course from what you think it should really be about, then be part of the solution. Be a head teacher. After all, it is the best job in the world.

Ian Gilbert, Craig-Cefn-Park (again), February 2014

Acknowledgements

So many people to thank:

Lucy and Toby, as you should never underestimate the power of unconditional love.

My family, for showing you can take people out of South London but you can't take South London out of people. #FamilyMatters

My other family – the remarkable students, families, staff and governors of Passmores Academy – for trusting me.

Ian Gilbert and Caroline Lenton for believing I had a book in me and then crowbarring it out.

The wonderful editor, Fiona Spencer Thomas, for taking on the challenge of pulling together my ramblings to make more sense.

My teachers, Frank Jennings, Mike Conboy, Steve Telfer, John Rothwell, John Hale, Dick Masters and E. A. D. Kingsbury, and all the others who helped keep me on the right path.

And Natalie Christie, Kevin Sadler, Catherine Anderson, Jon Clark, Stephen Drew, Susan Byrd, Jo Connolly, Russell King and Sheila Sumsion for covering my many weaknesses.

Introduction

I've been thinking about my reasons for wanting to write this book, and the prime reason is that it reflects my own love of my job as a head teacher. Working with young people is just the most fantastic career. I love encouraging children by saying things like, 'I want you to have a job like mine so you can wake up each day and look forward to enjoying it.' It's wonderful to know that you can make an impact on their lives. Have you seen the articles in newspapers in which someone says they owe their success to their wonderful teacher? I wanted to share that feeling of pride and encourage others to aspire to being a head.

It goes back to the summer of 2007, when I was in my first year as a head and attended the National College for School Leadership (NCSL) conference. At the time, Steve Munby was running the NCSL and Ben Page, of the market research company Ipsos MORI, was giving a keynote talk on the troubles ahead with regard to the recruitment of head teachers. He showed some slides which demonstrated that, by 2014, forty per cent of head teachers would have retired and there just weren't enough people wanting to be heads. He also quoted some statistics about the number of headships that had to be re-advertised and concerns about who would fill these important jobs in the future.

I couldn't get my head around it. Here I was in the auditorium, listening and thinking, 'Really?' I couldn't work it out. I don't think it was only because I'd just become a head myself. It was simply that I'd always wanted to be a head from the time I decided to be a teacher at the age of around twelve. I'd always wanted to be a head teacher because that, for me, was the top of the teaching profession. I wanted to be a teacher because I wanted to make an impact. I'd been very lucky with my role models at primary school, but particularly at secondary school, where I'd had brilliant teachers. They had helped this fairly normal council estate boy from South London down the right path, and now it was time to pay them back. I had always thought, 'How can I make the biggest difference to the most people?' and knew it was by becoming a head.

So, that is what led me to write this book and, hopefully, it will encourage other teachers to want to be heads too. Over the course of the last couple of crazy years, I've spoken to many trainee and newly qualified teachers (NQTs) from Teach First. I have been to Keele and Newcastle universities and I always ask PGCE students about to launch into their careers how many of them want to be heads. It's usually only a handful and generally they are male. If they are secondary school teachers, it's usually the PE teachers, arrogant so-and-sos that we all are! I don't get it. I don't understand why this is the case. It's not a criticism of those who don't want to do the job; it's just that it's what I have always wanted to do.

When I take on a role, I try to be the best I possibly can at it. I know it is possible to be a great classroom teacher, but this was more to do with striving to be at the top of my profession and, as far as I was concerned, that meant being a head. I've left every job feeling sad and tearful (I know, it's a great surprise that I'm such a softie!), thinking of the kids and the staff relationships I've left behind but, ultimately, it was always the right thing to do. I wanted to be a head by the time I was forty and spend time on the golf course at fifty-five. That was always the plan.

So, if I can write anything that makes people think, 'Actually, there's as much, if not more, joy as there is stress involved in being a head' and just one person picks up this book and reads even a snippet before they get bored, then it's been worth writing.

Part one

Chapter 1

If I Can Do It, Anyone Can

Long before the days of Channel 4's TV series *Educating Essex*, I was born and grew up on a council estate in Penge, South London, Penge sur Mer, the same place as the wonderful Phil Beadle. My dad was a plumber and I was the youngest of four with two elder brothers and a sister. For the first twelve years of my life, mum was at home looking after us and I went to the local Royston Primary School, where I did really well. I was always bright but not necessarily the most hardworking of pupils, which was a bit of a challenge for me. If it didn't involve sport or chasing a ball of one kind or another, I found motivation quite difficult. I was very fortunate that I had a teacher called Clive Streets, who was in charge of sport at the school, and to whom I owe a lot. He gave me the opportunity, at a very young age, of playing cricket, rugby, football and all sorts of sports that many primary schools didn't support at the time. I came from a sporty family, but school was really the start of my love affair with sport.

When it came to secondary school, I went to the local comprehensive. It had been the secondary modern school when my two brothers went there and that was where you went if you failed your 11-plus and didn't get into the local grammar school. By the time I arrived, that system didn't exist any more, so I just followed in my brothers' footsteps and went to the same school. I was very lucky because the school was tough; all boys, culturally diverse, testosterone laden and lots of them bussed out to the 'burbs from Inner London. It was full of sporty teachers as well as the PE staff, so it was a fantastic environment for me. I was sport mad and the difference at this school was that, if I wanted to stay on at school doing sport, that was encouraged. I owe a huge debt to Frank Jennings, who was the head of PE, and to John Rothwell, John Hale, Geoff Bevan and Dick Masters. They weren't necessarily PE teachers but they ran teams, and if I wanted to try out new things or practice, they would support me, whether it was before or after school. They really helped me understand mastery and how dedication and commitment can help you achieve your goals, an ethos that filters through other aspects of my life.

Frank, in particular, encouraged me to become a PE teacher by putting me through refereeing and coaching courses. By the time I left school at sixteen, I was already a referee in four different sports and was coaching six sports. So, I went on to study A levels at the local college, knowing where I wanted to be, knowing where I wanted to go, and I was pretty well qualified to start. That certainly was very evident at university, as I was well prepared with a good range of knowledge. I wasn't just a rugby player, I wasn't just a cricketer. I was able to turn my hand to lots of things and that stood me in good stead. I'll never forgot the debt that I owe those teachers, because they were just massive in encouraging me to do what I needed to do.

I guess teaching became a family thing. My two brothers and sister are all teachers, although we've all followed different routes. Big brother Trevor has now been a head for about three years. He loves his job too.

Middle brother Malcolm taught just outside Runcorn. He was very much caught up in the Hillsborough disaster, where a couple of the youngest who died on that tragic day were pupils at his school and in his class. Malcolm found that really difficult and it gave me a real insight into the emotional stresses involved in teaching, as Malcolm had to give up being a teacher. He loved it but he couldn't cope with the mourning that was going on around him and, at the time, the union really failed to support him. When the going is tough, what you need is the union to put an arm around your shoulder and say, 'It's OK, you need to get through this and we can help you.' There were times when life did get in the way of the job and he didn't get the support he needed. So, that's why he gave up being a teacher for thirteen or fourteen years but, I'm glad to say, he is now back teaching at a school in Cheshire.

Sister Tracey headed to grammar school, having passed her 11-plus. She did really well and is now head of humanities at a school in Somerset. This was all very unusual for a family whose parents were a plumber and a housewife. Obviously, there's a lot more to my mum than that, but both parents placed great importance on education and the schools we attended, They wanted them to be schools that met all our needs. I remember rolling my eyes at my head teacher on numerous occasions because he always referred to the importance of the 'family unit' at Kentwood School. I remember thinking, 'Oh God, this bloke's waffling on again about the family,' and yet, I hear myself saying the same thing all the time. I've lived with the awareness of what an impact school can have on children. It set me up and gave me structure.

Lots of friends I used to hang out with under the playground slide on the council estate took very different routes in life, and I suppose I was probably the 'boffin' among my mates. I was the one who was going to be a teacher and that aim stuck with me through to university. In my first year, we did some micro teaching that involved being videoed while you were teaching and watching it with a group of your peers. I remember listening to myself (it was one of my earliest recollections of hearing myself on tape) and thinking, 'Who is that common bloke? Who's that bloke who doesn't pronounce his aitches. He sounds a bit rough' and it was me. All the way through school, I had been the 'posh' one because I had aspirations to teach, my dad was the chair of governors, my mum ran the parent–teacher association and my brothers had gone to university. Around my friends and in my peer group, I was seen as a privileged person, until I went to a very middle-class university in Chichester where, suddenly, I wasn't. I was a bit of a rough diamond, which I guess would be the best description of me. It felt quite strange.

The teacher training journey was great. I was playing sport at a good level and could have gone to Loughborough, Exeter or another of those high profile sports universities, but I chose to go to Bishop Otter College in Chichester, which was then called the West Sussex Institute of Higher Education. There were a couple of reasons for my choice. First, the college was primarily interested in training me to become a teacher and not in the level of sport I'd played previously. This was really key because teaching is all I wanted to do. The playing side of it was great and I still love my sport, but it was all about my passion for teaching. I wanted to repay all those hours that all my teachers had invested in me through school. They had given me direction and nurtured me to be the young man I had become, so I was desperate to do them justice. I just knew that was where I needed to be.

The second factor that influenced my choice was the male-to-female ratio, which was one to seven and, having come from an all-boys school, that was quite significant. I seem to remember that the 'alternative' university prospectus gave you all the interesting bits of information, such as how many bars, social events and girls there were on campus, which probably influenced my choice, if I'm completely honest.

I did a good old-fashioned BEd PE course with maths as a second subject. I didn't have a maths A level, just government and politics, history, and economics, but they didn't offer any of those as a second subject. I avoided geography because I hated it, even though my geography teacher is a very good friend of mine from way back. So, I struggled through maths and it was a bit of a battle, but I was lucky because both my brothers were maths teachers, so I did have help at the end of the phone if I needed it. I scraped through. Basically, I had four years of doing my hobby, surrounded by other sporty people and I felt very fortunate to have made some amazing friends. In fact one, Jon Clark, ended up being my best mate through university, my best man at my wedding and is now my deputy head, replacing Mr Drew when he left to take up his own headship.

As I had always wanted to be a teacher, I didn't find the journey through university and teaching practice difficult. I remember the first week in my first real job at Angmering School, which is a great place with an excellent PE department on the south coast. A sixth-form boy squared up to me and, luckily, I remembered the advice I'd been given by Frank when I was doing some coaching at school. He told me that, if somebody does that, you should put both hands in your pockets and take one step back, so I did. He was just boundary pushing and testing the new bloke's reaction. I was twenty-two and he was eighteen and he didn't think he needed to do as he was told.

I was very lucky that I went into a PE department with two brilliant male PE staff as colleagues. Dave Yates was head of PE and Kevin Grant led the A level teaching. The female PE staff members were great too, but it was all quite segregated. Kevin and Dave trained me and nurtured me, giving me opportunities to develop my skills and match my weaknesses, both as a PE teacher in lessons but also in coaching at a good level, including national basketball. Being involved at that level was absolutely amazing.

Even though PE was my passion, I deliberately made a point of teaching maths as a second subject, because I was aware that, some day, when my knees gave way and my belly got too big, I would need it (and before anybody says anything, both those things have happened). This made me very saleable as a teacher. It would probably make me even more saleable now. The academic rigour of being a maths teacher and the alternative perspective of people seeing me in a different role in school had a really positive outcome.

After a couple of years at Angmering, I went to Cheam High School in South London, which was a struggling school. I remember a young man riding his motorbike down the middle of a corridor on one of my first days. Luckily, the school had a very driven, focused head teacher called John Vaughn, who was very 'old school'. Everyone was called by their surname and he had very strong views on what people should do. He was a bit of a dinosaur in some ways but, for me, this was great, and he was incredibly supportive.

I remember being interviewed for the job on a very hot summer's day and one of the candidates was wearing just a shirt and tie with no jacket. Our interviews lasted about forty minutes but his lasted just ten. One of the first questions he was asked was, 'I see you haven't got a jacket. Is there any reason why?' I think he replied with something along the lines of, 'Fashion … it's the fashion,' so his interview was short.

John Vaughn had very black-and-white views on many things but he loved his sport, particularly basketball. He was a statistician for a local national league basketball team, not that you'd ever guess it as he was slightly short and not someone you'd think was a basketball fan. I came in and, within a couple of years, we had an England basketball player in the school. I'd picked him up in Year 7 and worked with him. I did Saturdays, I did holidays, I ran basketball camps and got all the support I needed. What that taught me was that, if you just roll your sleeves up and get on with it, without asking for the money or recognition first, it does get noticed.

I was fortunate to have worked there, as I know from speaking to other professionals over the years, that this isn't always the case in other schools. Sometimes people feel unloved and that the 'extra' they put in isn't recognised, so I try really hard to make sure I appreciate my staff. However, there is a little bit of me that still niggles about colleagues who come into the profession and want to organise this or that but, once I have said, 'Yes, go for it,' they are really only interested in the pay. If you want to do something, get on with it and the recognition will come. I think that's something that has been lost over recent years because, ultimately, many of us are in the job because it is a job and we're getting paid for it, but it should also be something that you have a passion for.

I was lucky that, at Cheam High, I was recognised for getting on with it when I taught A level students. We had an association with the local tennis centre that attracted some of the top junior tennis players in Europe to the school. They spent most of their time playing tennis but I also taught them A level PE. It was fantastic to see the potential of these aspiring champions and how hard they worked on their game, although it was quite difficult getting them to concentrate on anything else. Who can blame them?

Chapter 2

Twitter Chatter

When I started to work on this book, I put out a tweet inviting teachers who didn't aspire to being a head to email me and tell me why. One reason came out above just about everything else, which annoyed me. In fact, it made me really angry. It was classroom teacher snobbery. That is the only way I can describe it. People were saying, 'Well, I came into the profession to improve children's lives by teaching, so I'm going to stay in the classroom and do just that.' When the emails started coming in, I just wanted to scream and say, 'Actually, I've got a massive classroom. I have over a thousand children in my lessons as well as over two hundred staff,' because, ultimately, the whole school is my classroom. I know that might sound a bit cranky, but that's the way it is.

Walking the walk and talking the talk as a head, sets the tone. It impacts enormously on others. I do many whole-school assemblies and really value them, though I know plenty of heads don't have the luxury of a space to do this. I value them because assemblies can be quick, can deliver one message or be about community, and you tell everybody at once. I do miss the personal touch, of course I do. What I miss more than anything else is being a form tutor and I still remember all my groups.

The longest I'd been at any school prior to coming to Passmores Academy in Harlow, was four years. In my second year, I'd picked up a tutor group in Year 7, which was Year 9 when I left, and before that I had a Year 11 group. We were based on the top floor of a three-storey school in South London and we had quite an authoritarian deputy. The brilliant Gail Tolley, who went on to be an outstanding head, used to be the uniform person and we had a rule about skirts having to be within an inch of the knee. Not surprisingly, the girls in my tutor group had the same magic walk that lots of girls have. As they walk, their skirts miraculously roll up at the top and, mysteriously, get shorter. It's a walk only teenage girls have managed to master, and they have mastered it well. On one occasion, I remember sitting at my desk taking the register and, looking out of the window, I spotted Miss Tolley marching up the path, with ruler in hand. I said to the girls, 'Right, I can't say that any of you have rolled up your skirts, but make sure that we're not letting each other down and we don't get Miss Tolley annoyed.' Of course, the skirts magically unrolled and were all very modest lengths when Miss Tolley came in. She thanked me very much for their correct uniform, congratulating them on how well they had done and off she went. Of course, the girls' skirts were probably not quite as long by the time they left the room, but it's just that sort of camaraderie that I miss. I miss the closeness. I miss being the person they go to for advice. I still have that to a degree, although I am aware that there's an element of distance now that I'm the head teacher and not their form tutor. Overall, I don't buy the 'I just want to be a classroom teacher because I really want to make a difference' or 'I don't want to go to the dark side' attitude.

As a PE teacher, you can imagine all my PE mates telling me I was moving to the 'dark side' when I moved into assistant headship. I don't feel like that at all. I believe that I'm more central now than I've ever been, because it's not just the kids I teach that I make a difference to, it's everybody, staff and students. Sometimes I wish I could just turn up, teach my lessons, do my marking and leave at the end of the day. The amount of time that is taken up by the HR issues of adults and children alike, makes me miss that a little, but not enough to think I don't want to be a head.

So, yes, I was peeved to get that negative email feedback from my tweet, even though I understand where they're coming from. I just don't think those individuals are seeing it from my angle or from a head's point of view. It's the absolute joy of the job, of seeing something that you set up, that you've guided and allowed to develop, of putting systems in place that mean somebody else can help these young people be wonderful and fulfil their dreams. I'm not certain whether I had more joy getting fantastic GCSE results from my class or from that glow you get when you see young people interacting successfully with an adult. The vicarious pleasure I get when I see someone I've employed because I thought they'd be brilliant and would bring the best out in the kids, is immeasurable.

It is a bit paternal, I suppose, like standing back and watching as your children do lovely things and grow into good people. It gives me that double-bubble feeling. I see adults I have employed, worked with and encouraged making a difference to young people and their lives being lit up as a result. I think that is probably what gives me the most satisfaction professionally. So, I've never understood the negativity. The most important thing I want to get over is that, just because you're not in a classroom, it doesn't mean you're not a teacher. I still feel that I'm a teacher first but one who has to do all the books and admin as well. I will never lose sight of the fact that I'm a teacher. I love being a teacher and I always will be, lottery win or no lottery win.

Chapter 3

The Great TV Experiment

We'd better cover the *Educating Essex* years, I guess. 'So, how did it come about?' you might ask and I am asked this often. It was March 2010, and I had a call from reception saying, 'Channel 4's on the line, they'd like to talk to you.' Now, normally I would say, 'I'll pass on that thanks. Take a message and I'll get back to them some time, never.' However, this was on the back of a term when there had been a bit of a different flavour to the school.

When there is grief and in troubled times, people tend to pull together and that's certainly where we had been for a term as, sadly, just prior to Christmas, one of our young men, Jamie Bone, passed away. It was a surprise to all of us. His cousin, Brooke, knocked on my office door and came in very upset. She told me that Jamie had just died. I didn't really know what to say. I just looked at her, thinking, 'That can't be true. I only saw him the other day and he was as right as rain.'

Jamie was a young man who was born with some challenges, from a learning point of view, but he also had some physical problems, including a heart defect. He'd attended the local primary school, just around the corner from Passmores, where he had struggled. His health had had a big impact on his learning and the amount of time he could spend in school but, at secondary school he'd been considerably better. It had a lot to do with strength and puberty but, ultimately, he'd been a really happy member of our community.

He was a very joyful character and one of those kids that every-body liked. He was popular with the staff and always ready with a smile and a chat, usually about football. He was just one of life's radiators and one of those people who made you feel better for seeing him. He would often be in reception, because his mum and dad picked him up and dropped him back, so I'd manufacture a reason to go there just to see him, to have a chat and see how his day had gone.

On the day when Brooke knocked on my door it was very difficult. I really couldn't believe it and it's not the sort of thing you can phone a parent to confirm. We just had to wait and try to find out from other people in the family whether it was true or not. It was difficult on many levels, the main one being that he'd been such an integral part of the school and we could see that he had really blossomed.

Jamie's parents asked whether the funeral procession could come via the school on the way to the crematorium and, of course, we said yes. On that grey, rainy and cold English day in December, I found myself standing outside the old Passmores building with a thousand young people and staff waiting for Jamie to pass. It was extremely humbling to see the respect and care that the students had for him and how they just stood there in absolute silence, waiting patiently until the funeral procession arrived and drove into the school, pulling up outside the reception area where Jamie used to wait for his parents, before turning around and heading to the crematorium. There, we had students making a guard of honour and reading a poem at the service.

We then had a term of talking to the students about Jamie and how he was missing out on the chances they were having. It resonated with some of them, especially those who weren't taking up their opportunities to learn, to represent the school and to value themselves. We were able to talk about the fact that they should feel privileged to have that opportunity because others, like Jamie, don't and they should grab those chances, out of respect for those who aren't so lucky.

When Channel 4's phone call came, it would have been disingenuous of me not to talk to them. We're always telling the students to live their lives and not be afraid of taking risks, but to weigh up their options carefully and engage with those situations. For me to say that the school was not going to do the same would have been wrong, so I said yes. David Clews, the director of the series, arranged to meet me, along with Grace, the producer/director. I drove off to Harlow Town on the day we'd arranged to meet but they weren't there. They'd forgotten that I'd arranged to pick them up, so they were already in a cab on their way to Passmores and we missed each other, which wasn't the best of starts. I have to say I was cursing a bit but I got back and met them and they were absolutely lovely.

We sat in my office (if you've watched the series, you'll have seen it – it's where I hold my leadership team meetings) and they described the show they had in mind. I wasn't really aware that it was a series at the time but thought it was a fly-on-the-wall documentary that would include some filming in our school using fixed-rig cameras. They were talking about it being filmed half in school and half out of school. They would follow the students and their social lives and find out how that impacted on them at school. My initial response was to say, 'I can't make this decision. It's too close and will have too much of a direct effect on me. I need to talk to my governors.' So that's what we did.

I had at that point, however, given David a warning. I looked him in the eye and let him know that, if anyone were to do any harm to my school, my students, my staff or me, I would find him. I come from a council estate in South London and I know some people who have rather different moral standards than my own, so he was likely to find himself underneath a motorway extension if he did anything wrong! Now, I'm not particularly proud of that conversation, but there you go. We had it and I was going to get it straight there and then. David looked me in the eye and said that, if it was to go ahead and it worked, then we would walk away as friends and remain friends afterwards, but the only chance we had of that happening was if the series was fair.

The governing body met and they formed a little working group who met David and Andrew Mackenzie, from the production company Twofour, to discuss the plan. The working group then deliberated, went back to the governors and suggested that we took part. It wasn't a unanimous decision. There were a couple of governors who thought it was a bad idea and voted against it, but it was fairly convincing. I think it was about fifteen or sixteen to two in favour.

Then the hard work began for the governors. They met again to look through the contract that described what was to happen and what control we had. Obviously, we had no control whatsoever. No commercial TV company was going to give us editorial control, because they wanted to tell a story. The governors were particularly interested in protecting the students, the staff and the school's reputation. Of course that was never going to be at risk, as David reiterated his promise that we would finish up as friends. He also said the governors would be proud of what they had achieved as Channel 4 had no intention of doing a hatchet job on the school.

The governors were very focused on safeguarding and ensuring that the young people featured would be well supported by child psychologists and that all the staff and students in the school would be consulted as to whether they wished to take part, which would be down to Twofour to organise. I deliberately chose not to be the person to send letters to parents because I'm very fortunate to have a lot of loyalty in the community and I didn't want to cause any upset. The vast majority of parents and students, though not all, are very loyal to the school and very loyal to me. They've chosen to send their young people to Passmores on the back of its reputation and, after coming to the school and listening to its head teacher's open evening talk. They decided, even after they'd listened to me, that I'm the right person to help bring up their most precious gifts, so we're very, very protective of them.

The programme was set in motion. Consultation letters went out and only a couple of students didn't want to be involved. Twofour dealt with all the documentation and handled all the administrative matters. This proved really helpful in the future as, when I received a Freedom of Information Act request from some journalists keen to dig dirt, I couldn't give them what they wanted because it was held by Twofour and

Channel 4, and they are not public bodies and therefore not obliged to supply any information.

Once the negotiations were complete and the contract signed, Twofour spent some time in and around the school during the summer term, focussing on one year group. A couple of lovely researchers spent time getting to know the students really well. The members of staff who spent time with them also came to trust them. So, by September, when they would start filming, Twofour had a very good idea as to which students they wanted to follow and who would be an interesting character with a possible a storyline.

At the start of the September term, the fixed-rig cameras weren't in, as the plan was to install them during half-term in October. So, on the first morning of the first day back at school, I walked into the sports hall for our whole-school assembly, followed closely by a TV crew with three hand-held cameras. It was odd, and I can't say it was particularly enjoyable. It just felt strange. However, when I got going, standing in front of those thousand children and two hundred staff members, talking about the start of the year and what it meant and what work had to be done, it was very easy to forget them because, ultimately, the children deserved my complete attention and that's what they got.

After half-term, we came back to a school filled with lots of cameras. Fixed-rig cameras, the size of a football (like the ones used in *One Born Every Minute* and *Big Brother*), along with ambient mikes, were erected around the school in selected classrooms, corridors and offices. For example, there were four cameras and lots of hanging mikes in my office. On the way into the school, we were handed a microphone to wear and that just became part of the pattern. At first we were all conscious that the cameras were there but, very soon, they were forgotten and both students and staff behaved naturally.

It is important to remember that this was not something we'd seen on TV before and there was no comparable series we could watch, so life just went on. I wasn't particularly aware of the specific stories that were being followed as, even though there were over sixty cameras there, three of them were recording at any one time and there were no red lights on them to indicate which were live. It was all very natural and unstaged.

The original plan had been to follow the students in and out of school. The production company realised very quickly that, unfortunately, teenagers outside school are quite dull. They spend most of their time doing very little, often looking down at one electronic device or another and there wasn't much of a story to follow there. I wasn't aware of it at the time, but evidently they filmed less and less outside school over the course of the year and focused more on the school activities.

It was very bizarre, therefore, to come back in the tail half of the year to be told that Twofour had a rough copy of an episode ready for us to watch. I went to the hotel over the road, along with some governors and those members of staff who were going to be featured, to sit in a darkened room and watch the very first cut of Episode 1. Anyone who watched the series will know that this episode is very focused on the deputy head, Mr Drew, and a couple of our challenging young people, including an accusation against him that he'd struck a student.

It was bizarre to watch because it was our little school and I was looking at it in a way that I didn't normally view it and I was worried. The first episode immediately revealed how little filming had been done outside school. I was also concerned that it was very focused on Steve Drew and how vulnerable that made him. It doesn't take Einstein to work out how fond I am of Steve and how much I owe him for his hard work with me over the course of ten years, and I was reluctant to put him in that position. It would have been fine if it was me, as I was part of the decision-making process, but not for him.

We did ask for some minor changes to be made because I wanted to make sure the programme covered the whole school journey and it was important to represent that correctly. There are many incidents and difficult scenarios involving young people at school. If something challenging happened, and obviously it was going to and did, you have to make some difficult choices, so it was important that they included the whole picture. It was fine to show that children sometimes don't do as they're told, and I'm not certain any of us think they do, but the show needed to demonstrate that we were determined to work with the children, overcome whatever challenges arose and progress together. As long as they showed that complete journey, including any bridges that needed building and the outcomes, we'd feel comfortable and confident that we had done a decent job.

Almost all the programmes that we saw in rough edit did that. Apart from some minor points, the process went quite smoothly. For example, we were uncomfortable with some comments that hadn't been heard by anyone else. As the school wasn't able to react to them, we didn't think they should be included. We felt it was wrong that people might make judgements on the school based on remarks over which we had no control.

There were some very difficult programmes to watch, for example, in Episode 2 where there was some cyber-bullying between a couple of girls, including our friend Carrie, half of Carrie 'n' Ashleigh. I found that one of the least engaging episodes in the series, contrary to most of the female staff who found it the most interesting. I think that's probably to do with the complete drain on time that is caused by girls' friendship group issues and them falling out. Those teachers who have dealt with these issues will know that you can spend hours of your life listening to, 'She said this' and 'She said that'. You deal with it and arrive at a resolution and they say, 'OK, it's fine, we'll move on.' Then the next day, you'll see them best friends again, skipping down the corridor. It feels like you've just wasted a day of your life. That's why that particular episode was the only one where I got out my phone while it was being screened.

The first edit of Episode 3, featuring Vinni, which I watched sitting in the Park Inn in Harlow, was really dark. For those who know the programme, it's the episode in which Vinni is taken into care. The final cut was still very uncomfortable to watch but, had people seen the first edit, they would have been very upset to see Vinni so alone in the children's home where he had decided he wanted to be. It was tough, at least that's how it felt to me. It seemed like it was a really dark time for him and I felt hopeless and helpless. When I watched the first edit of the episode, I was fine to let it go because that's how grim it felt. Afterwards, when it went to Channel 4 for their first screening, they decided it was just too dismal. In fact, the feedback was, 'If we show people this, they'll be feeling so miserable, they'll never want to come back to watch the next episode.' So they tried to lighten it a bit and make it less full of doom and gloom, even though, if I'm honest, that was the reality of Vinni's situation at the time.

As we were watching the episodes being pulled together, what became really clear to me was that we needed to get the viewers to the end of the journey. If they reached the last episode, they would see that, despite the challenges and despite the children's occasional inability to make the right choices, without pushing the self-destruct button, they could make it. If we kept going, bringing the young people with us, eventually they would reach the end of their journey into adulthood armed with the skills and opportunities to move on, leaving our school as decent young people and making a worthwhile life for themselves. Our influence and the effects of encouraging them to achieve their potential became very evident in Episode 7, the last episode. I know I talk about the journey a lot but it's important that people understand the process of educating children. It's a rite of passage that we, as teachers, can influence and support.

I have been asked numerous times what I was paid for the series. The answer is nothing, zero, never have been, didn't want to be and didn't even ask. In reality, I think the final episode was the payment. That episode included the culmination of the Vinni story, which was tough and included us not allowing him to go to his prom or leavers' day. That was one of the most difficult decisions I've ever made but was the right thing to do, even though Vinni was down and struggling and life outside was giving him a bit of a kicking. Vinni hadn't earned the right to be there or celebrate the end of his passage through school, because he hadn't invested in it. What Vinni had done, at times, was to make his life better by making other people's lives worse, and that isn't good enough. Young people have to understand that their happiness shouldn't be dependent on somebody else being miserable.

The other half of the final episode was about Ryan Carr, who has Asperger's. He is an amazing young man who had come to our school because of some sad circumstances. He'd been living in Spain where he'd been kept back in a primary school, but had to return to the UK with his family. Much to his mum's shock, we put him straight into the right year group for his age where he'd flourished and blossomed and become a happy young man. He smiled when you saw him and it was lovely to see the awe and wonder in his eyes, which made us pleased to have him at our school.

The best part of it was our delight at seeing how the other students treated him. They didn't laugh at him but laughed with him and they joined in with his awful human beatboxing and didn't judge him. That's what we want for our school. As we say to our students all the time, exam results are really important as they will open the door to an interview but it's you, the human being, who will get that job. Also, how does a person go from working in or for a team to leading a team? Well, that's not down to exam results. That is due to an ability to empathise, to understand the other people in your team and to put yourself in their shoes, attributes that don't appear in any league table. To see the students of Passmores understanding Ryan, appreciating that he's going to want to sing as he walks down the corridor and sometimes say 'hello' in an excited way, was amazing.

Obviously, we knew the production company had filmed the leavers' assembly and Ryan's impromptu decision to speak. I was surprised when a couple of people accused us of rigging the event. They obviously don't know students who have the challenge of Asperger's, because what is in Ryan's head comes out of Ryan's mouth. As we would say, the hashtag filter doesn't really exist. So, it was only Ryan who chose to make his speech. There were parts in that episode that I hadn't seen, including the one where Ryan is sitting outside the hall talking about school and the family that we were to him. He is saying how scared he is to be leaving and that I was an inspiration to him. That just blew me away.

Even now, it makes me emotional. For anybody to say that you're an inspiration, and that your influence has made him or her a better person, is a compliment beyond words. It's probably the second biggest compliment anybody could pay me. The first is when a parent shows their child around Passmores on an open evening and, having sat through my waffle (which I plan to take twenty minutes but usually lasts about forty-five), they still think Passmores is the place to help them bring up their child. It's a bit bewildering, if I'm honest, because I've got a boy and I know how trusting anybody with him is a huge decision for me. To make that choice about a school after visiting Passmores, watching lessons and hearing me talk, is basically saying, 'I trust you to help raise our child with our family's morals and I trust you to serve our child well.' Apart from that one, Ryan calling me an inspiration was just mind blowing and humbling.

Chapter 4

The Aftermath

The series came and went, with a variety of different horror stories along the way but I certainly hadn't expected the *Daily Mail* to turn up in reception the morning after the first episode aired. They wanted an interview and wouldn't take no for an answer, despite me telling them many times that it was up to Channel 4 to handle the national media. I was happy to deal with the local media, as I was only interested in local feedback. After all, it's their readers and listeners who are the people who choose to send their children to Passmores, not someone living in the north of England, Scotland or anywhere else.

You may have seen it or, if not, you can Google 'Daily Mail and Passmores Academy' to read what they had to say about me, which is forgivable. However, what they had to say about my young people is unforgivable. Thank goodness for the right-minded people who inundated their website with 'No, you've got it wrong' comments. The first twelve hours after the show were really difficult, because I'd read the article online and, for the first time in my school life, I ended up feeling that my job was all about me. It felt like a decision we'd made had made the staff, the students and the school vulnerable, as well as me. That morning I delivered the world's worst in-service training (INSET) day to staff on performance management review and appraisals. I didn't actually know the first episode was going to be broadcast the night before, so it was just luck that we had a training day.

If I'm really honest, I didn't think anyone would watch it. As far as I was concerned, it was just a documentary about a very normal school doing what normal schools do, up and down the country. They serve their children, irrespective of the baggage they bring or the hurdles they have to jump. The schools and teachers help them through it, supported by co-educators, learning support assistants, dinner ladies and cleaners. That is what happens in schools everywhere, which is why I never thought anyone would be interested. So, I wasn't prepared for the attention from national newspapers and, certainly, I wasn't expecting the negativity that came out in the first couple of days. Who could hate Passmores? Who could despise a school for trying to do its best for the students and community it serves? Every day we do the best we can and, if the best isn't good enough, people won't send their children to the school. If it is, the children will come. That's the bottom line.

Having got through that, and similar treatment in *The Sun* the following Saturday, I was relieved to receive the supportive emails that came in, and thank goodness for *The Guardian*. After the *Mail* and *Sun*'s hatchet jobs, *The Guardian* sent along an amazing journalist, Emine Saner. She met Steve and me and spent the day in school. I think she was probably a little bit blown away by the tidal wave of stories about our school and the passion and commitment we had for it. She was impressed by the fact that we were going to defend Passmores with our dying breath, against her or anybody else who wanted to say something detrimental.

While she was here, a fire alarm went off. We were in the new building by then and the alarm was a bit flaky and prone to causing unintended fire drills, which wasn't ideal with a national news journalist on site. We had to traipse out across the field for the drill, even though it was unplanned. Fortunately, as always, our fire drill was exceptional as the staff as well as the students know exactly what their responsibilities are. It was great to watch, so that would have impressed her too. She wrote a lovely article about the school and the students, just from our perspective.

Email after email came in and all but a small handful were positive. There were a few that said things like, 'Why are you bothering with those young people who don't want to learn?' and 'Why don't you just lock them in a room at the start of day and let them out at the end?' I politely replied to these with, 'Thank you, I'll give your email the due consideration it deserves,' and promptly binned them.

By contrast, we had many emails from people saying kind things like, 'I wish I'd had teachers like you when I was at school.' They probably did but hadn't realised it at the time because you don't necessarily see that as a child. There were positive comments from young people, as well as families and teachers. One of the most heart-warming things about the experience was how many parents emailed to say, 'It's the first time we've been able to sit down with our teenage children and watch a programme we could all discuss as a family.'

I got a few emails from Passmores' parents who were worried. A couple had been on to blogs and written some ridiculous things. It wasn't entirely unfair, because all the events had happened as they were shown, but they represented only a tiny minority of the daily incidents in the school. Obviously, the programme was heavily edited to focus on the most exciting of these episodes to make good viewing, which may have given parents cause for alarm. Yes, we have some challenging students, as does every school, but the vast majority turn up every day, do the right thing and leave. To focus entirely on these well-behaved students might be a bit like watching them text messaging. As well as the emails, there was Twitter.

We were fairly new to it when our 'Twitter moment' happened and, suddenly, we had thousands of followers rather than three, two of whom were probably family members and the other was Steve following me, and me following him.

As the series progressed, the messages continued. Then the awards started to come. It was awesome going to the BAFTAs (David Clews won an award for directing the series) and attending different events up and down the country at which people said they were blown away by what teachers do. Walking down the red carpet behind some really famous people and waiting to hear the winning names (knowing that we probably hadn't made it) was amazing. I even stood next to Alan Carr having a wee, which was very weird! Afterwards, at dinner with Jay Hunt, the creative director of Channel 4, Jon Snow came up to say to us, 'What you do is remarkable and don't forget that, you should be very proud of yourselves and thank you and your other teachers for everything you do.' It's Jon Snow, for heaven's sake! He does proper journalism and proper TV, and he was saying those lovely things to us!

Then, unbelievably, I was asked to present an award at the British Comedy Awards. I remember the limo turning up at home to take Drewy and me to the ceremony. We drove to where I think *The X Factor* live shows are filmed and got out of the car to walk down the blue carpet behind Jeff Goldblum, who recognised us and said hello. We then went backstage where everyone, including Vic Reeves and Bob Mortimer, was having a drink and I thought 'Why the hell are we here?' Then we were collected by our chaperone, the person who makes sure you're in the right place at the right time, who told us that we should be in the green room. We'd avoided it as we thought we shouldn't be in there, drinking with all those incredibly famous people. But no, we were shown through to a separate room to join the presenters of the awards. We walked into a very strange scenario to see people like Barbara Windsor, Freddie Starr, Amir Khan and Mark Wright, and for them to recognise us was extraordinary. Even more amazing was the moment when Barbara Windsor made a beeline for us to talk about her life in school and how grateful she was for what it had done for her.

In the audience, I sat beside Paul Merton and Robbie Coltrane, surrounded by other famous people including Victoria Wood and, of course, Barbara Windsor. During the course of that evening, Victoria Wood came up and asked to have a photograph taken with us, saying she was honoured to be in a picture taken with two teachers. It was lovely to chat to her. It was all just crazy!

I won't forget sitting at the table and a TV director leaning over and saying, 'You do understand that this is all garnish. What you see here isn't real; it's what *you* do that matters.' It was obvious to him that I was very nervous, because it was live TV and I was going to present an award. He also said that everybody in the room had a personality disorder, otherwise they wouldn't be there. I think he said it to be kind but I presumed he meant us as well! It was very strange to be a schoolteacher following Vince Cable on to the stage to present an award and to have the presenter, Jonathan Ross, asking us about our school. Afterwards, I had a chat with him and his wife, Jane, and she said such lovely things about Jonathan enjoying the series and that he was really pleased to meet us.

It was completely unexpected and quite uncomfortable at times. I think Drewy was always a bit more at ease with it all than I was. He's now got an agent and another series coming out on Channel 4, but for me, it was more of a challenge, even though you can't really tire of being given these unexpected and exciting opportunities in life. I understand how people who chase reality TV or go on *Big Brother* can get addicted. It's not something that's ever going to happen to me, though, because I love my job and things that take me away from that role are sometimes a burden. So, I try to make sure that anything I do fits around school and I'm not off doing daytime television instead, even though I've been asked on numerous occasions. Being at school is the time when I'm doing the thing I love the most. The balance was easy to keep, because there was no temptation bigger than the temptation to be at school with our students, doing what I needed to do for them. It was certainly a very peculiar year.

Of course, things have moved on. Channel 4 did come back, very kindly, to ask if we'd do another series. They pushed hard but nicely. The governors met and we spoke about it. The little steering group and leadership team voted on whether we wanted to do another series. The vote was split. I didn't think it was the right thing to do, nor did the majority of my leadership team. Mr Drew was quite keen to do another series, as was Mr King (he's 'Clear off, scumbags' for those who know the intro) and one of the governors who is involved in PR. He just couldn't work out how he spends all his life trying to get these opportunities for his clients and we were turning down one that was gift-wrapped.

What did we have to gain from doing another series? It's going to sound wrong when I say that we got away with it, but I definitely felt there was an element of that. Twofour could have edited a very different show and portrayed the school very differently. They could have focused on negative situations as there are times when you don't handle things as well as you could or when you come into work a bit grumpy and not on top of your game. However, the production team chose to try and show the parts that were realistic and human and, hopefully, representative of who we are most of the time. So, what was there to gain? Money? Well, the school was offered money to do another series, but what was the benefit?

The other point was that the cameras had only just come down and our students and staff had lived with them for a long time. I was afraid the students would behave differently if we were to do it again so soon. Let me present a scenario. I have (let's call him) Billy, who's kicking off and not very happy in class. He storms out and I am nearby and miked up in front of a camera. Billy, instead of allowing me to de-escalate the situation by talking him through it, which would normally be the case, chooses to go for his fifteen minutes of fame and act up to the camera by being aggressive. In that case, we've made a mistake by putting a price on that young person's education which outweighs his interests.

Then there's the lovely Jay Hunt, from Channel 4, who has been just amazing, both during the series and since. She told me she had an issue with me and I wondered what it was. This is what she said: 'The big problem, Vic, is that however much money we offer the school to do another series, you're going to say "no" because, unfortunately for us, you have morals and scruples, which is not always the case in the TV world.' Despite her comment, we knew it was the right decision not to put the school back in the spotlight.

I think Thornhill Community Academy was brave to become involved in the series *Educating Yorkshire*, as they knew what to expect after seeing *Educating Essex* and still went ahead. I was very privileged to be invited up to the school by the head, Jonny Mitchell, to meet the staff, the governors and some students to talk about our experience. They wanted to know how it felt and what pitfalls they should avoid and I was able to fill them in from our experience. The only thing I've ever been able to say about the production company, Twofour, and specifically the people involved, David, Beejal-Maya, Grace, Gemma, Hamish and all the others behind the scenes, was that they have been absolutely true to their word and listened to our concerns. They did not always bow to them and they put a case up for some of the things they wanted to keep. We let some of these go because they fitted the story but it was always a compromise. They were honest, good people and we could tell Jonny that. I think he would agree with me.

It was incredible TV and there could be a BAFTA on its way, specifically for their last episode with Musharaf, known affectionately as Mushy P, and Matt as the focal points. I sobbed my little heart out all the way through. I feel really privileged to have been able to be part of their journey in a small way and, hopefully, to have prepared them a little for what was to come. I look on that series with such pride because they're just teachers like the rest of us, and I'm pleased to have made a contribution and been given the opportunity to help.

Since the series, I've been asked to talk at some major conferences in front of thousands of school leaders from around the world. I've also been invited to some brilliant places like Newcastle University, to talk to their PGCE students. I've given evidence to the Education Select Committee and been invited to all-party political groups in Westminster to talk about bullying. I've also been working with the Diana Award and the fantastic Alex Holmes on anti-bullying projects, which has been remarkable.

It has been a crazy time but my focus remains on Passmores. My love for the place is as strong as ever. However, the experience has unlocked some doors and given me opportunities I would never have had before and I'm very grateful for that. I guess in some ways *Educating Essex* has been quite a remarkable, positive, challenging and life-changing experience. It has shaped who I am and it's nice to feel that I've still got a voice and can speak up for the normal school, the normal head and normal teachers.

I now look at myself and find it very surprising that I've managed to move from a council estate in South London through secondary school, to being a head teacher and helping a new generation of young people. I was fortunate indeed to be in the right place and supported by the right people and am happy that I am able to give something back.

Chapter 5

'I Don't Want to be a Head Teacher'

I said that I'd try to cover some of the things that deter teachers from wanting to be a head teacher. Having spoken to teachers up and down the country, it has been quite alarming to discover just how few want to be heads. They don't seem to aspire to the job at the start or during their career. All they see are the reasons against it.

I've already covered the inverse snobbery of the 'I just want to be a classroom teacher' attitude, but there are other reasons too. Right now, a lot of heads are feeling huge pressure and that pressure is a deterrent to their deputies and others who may aspire to a headship. It appears that Ofsted is being used as a weapon to realise the government's drive for academies and to push a specific political viewpoint on what schooling and education should be about. The stress of the job is sometimes very intense. I'm not certain how many people realise just how much pressure heads are under and how this has increased. If I'm honest about my own job, it has become more of an emotional strain because so much of it involves coping with other people's difficulties. As a head teacher, I know the buck stops with me. If something goes wrong or a parent is irate or unhappy for some reason, it's likely that, when all other routes have been exhausted, it will arrive at my door. That brings emotional strain.

There is pressure throughout the school system. There is pressure on the classroom teacher or NQT who is still trying to find their feet and work out who they are; there is the pressure on someone who is aspiring to be head of department or to improve themselves; there is the pressure on a head of department, not only to hold colleagues to account for their results but also to be a supportive head of department; and there is the pressure on everybody to achieve good exam results.

The hardest I've ever worked was when I was head of department as the role is incredibly challenging. However, what is very evident for departmental heads is their stress around exam entries and making sure students fulfil their potential. As a head, I don't do that directly, I rely on them to do that. Therefore, I know that I'm putting pressure on them too.

As I've moved through from being an assistant head, deputy head to head, I don't feel I've seen a huge increase in pressure. It's just different, and it shouldn't be given as a specific reason for not wanting to do the job. As we've seen, if you're a teacher, you're under pressure anyway. Also, I now have excellent support networks around me that I didn't have as a head of department. I have a fantastic PA who looks after my diary and makes sure I'm in the right place, at the right time and with the right materials. I have a leadership team that does everything it can to filter stuff before it reaches me, and it backs me up as well as other staff. Consequently, I'm much more supported now than I've been at any other stage of my working life. I don't want to belittle other people but, if they think that undue demands are a good enough reason not to be a head, I think they're being unrealistic about their own pressures.

Not being ruthless enough is another reason I've heard mentioned for teachers not wishing to become heads. This came up in an appraisal conversation I had with my now deputy, Natalie Christie. As I do in all appraisal meetings, I discuss the staff member's aspirations and where they are in their journey through their professional life. I think it was probably Natalie's first appraisal as my deputy when, obviously, I asked, 'Do you want to become a head?' She looked me square in the eye, and it still bugs me, she knows it bugs me, and said, 'Oh no, I'm not ruthless enough to be a head.' My response was, 'What? But I'm a teddy bear. What are you talking about? I'm not ruthless.' She continued to look at me very directly and, with a tiny curl of her lip that spread into a smile, she said, 'You are, Vic. You're ruthless, as you'll do what you need to.'

It upset me to think that was how I was viewed but, ultimately, I will do what's right for the young people I serve. That's what drives me. I will make the difficult decision that may produce casualties along the way. There are people whose egos might get bruised or who think it was the wrong decision but, in the morning, I can look at myself in the mirror and know that what I've done is, in my opinion, the best thing for the children, the staff and the community. Clearly, it's normally about the kids, but I'm acutely aware that we all need to work together and that the teaching and admin staff, the cleaners and everybody else are part of the school's make-up and an all-important cog in the machine that is the school. In the end, the kids always come first and that is the way it has to be.

So, I guess I can be hard-nosed. I can make the hard decisions, but so would anybody else who knew they had to do what was right; so, for that reason, it doesn't feel ruthless. It feels necessary and that is something I hold on to. Sometimes it is tough and you're going to have to have that difficult conversation (or what is called the 'courageous conversation') with a member of staff, but actually it's okay, because I'm doing it for the right reasons. I'm doing it to support a young person, therefore I can sleep at night without it being a problem.

Another perceived obstacle is the loneliness and isolation of being a head teacher. I think teachers who fear this are right to a degree. There is isolation when you become a head. There is the 'them and us' scenario, because when you become a head, you're no longer one of the 'us'. I hope that I'm still a little bit of us, a 'thus' maybe, but it is different from being an assistant head or a deputy head. An assistant head is a member of the teaching staff. People go to them because they think they've got the ear of the head and, therefore, a conduit of information. The same goes for deputies. Of course, I've had the silent routine when entering a staffroom, which I'm sure any head or leader in a school will also have experienced.

When I finally reached my goal of becoming a head, I remember so clearly the first time I walked into the head's office with my name on the door, sitting at my desk, puffing out my chest and thinking, 'Right, this is it, Vic. You've aspired to being a head ever since you knew you wanted to be a teacher. Here you go.' I think what probably made it more daunting, but also better in a funny kind of way, is that Kevin Sadler, the previous head to whom I owe so much, had cleared out the office and left just one piece of paper on the notice board opposite my desk. It read, 'Remember, Vic, you make the weather,' which is a phrase that we'd used for a number of years. It's the barometer that determines how emotionally literate the staff are and how happy we all are, and it depends on the head getting the school's ethos right.

It was such a weird feeling to be there. It was during the holidays, in January, before school started and I thought, 'If it goes wrong, Vic, you've only got yourself to blame, mate.' It's a tough job, but I'm lucky to be part of a family of teachers, so I can pick up the phone to my brothers and sister and vent a bit. I think I was also lucky because Kevin knew he was going for a while, which enabled me to appoint my own leadership team from scratch soon after I became head. I deliberately appointed only internal candidates in deputy and assistant head jobs. This sent out a really important message. Passmores had been on a rocky journey since 2000/2001 when it should have failed its Ofsted inspection, and it continued to do so, until the start of my headship when we started improving and pushing to be outstanding. It was important that the staff realised that if you work hard you get rewards. That's why I appointed my lovely team from within. Very quickly, it made life so much easier because they already knew who I was and what I believed in. It took a lot less time than I anticipated for them to go through the storming, forming, norming and performing cycle to us all working in the same direction for the benefit of the children.

Yes, there is loneliness in the job, but only if I want it to be that way. I don't have to sit alone in my office doing reams of paperwork when there are people who are so much better at it than me, like my PA. I try to put more into what I'm good at, which is people generally, getting out and trying to create energy, which I see as one of my key tasks. I get out and about and I talk to the students. I'm present at breaktimes and lunchtimes, I drop in on lessons and I am around the school generally. I think that any loneliness comes from the feeling of responsibility, but how can you be lonely with, in my case, a school of 1,200 students? There is always somebody willing to have a chat, so isolation is not a major issue for me and it certainly shouldn't be something that puts people off becoming a head.

This leads into one of the biggest difficulties that people do have with being a head. It's the work–life balance. There is a lot of negativity about having what I call 'headship time' or the space to stop, think and reflect. I'll be honest, I still haven't got this right. The work–life balance is difficult. I know the way I work isn't necessarily how others work and it may very well not be sustainable in the long run as, when I get older, it will probably become more exhausting. I'm now in my (I was going to say early forties but that's probably pushing my luck!) mid-forties and I survive on fewer hours of sleep than I probably should but I still manage to find that 'headship time'. I don't work until my son has gone to bed and I try not to work too much until my wife has gone to bed. That does mean I work later into the evening or night. The main problem is that I'm one of those blinkered people who, once they have their mind on a train of thought, need to get it done, so I focus on it until it is done.

Getting the balance right is the toughest challenge, but I think I'm becoming more efficient and better at it. However, it's a big job, so getting a supportive governing body which understands that you need time off and you don't need to be continually churning out reams of paperwork that have no real benefit to the school can be a great help. There are lots of examples of individuals who do this better than I do but, at the moment, it's working for me.

Sometimes I look at my workload and remember the Year 6 teacher with the large class and all that marking to do, especially with what is expected in terms of feedback these days. Then there's the English or music teacher who's the only teacher of their subject in the school and who must feel both lonely and under pressure. The work–life balance isn't great in the teaching profession generally, and I can't hide the fact that it's also true in the world of the head, but it's not unmanageable. It just needs tinkering with at times. I think everyone needs to be reminded that they have families and homes to go to and that investment in family time is essential.

For me, one of the most important things about the work–life balance is being able to be at my son's events. If he comes first on sports day, for example, I want to be there to see it and that is important for us both. I have the same policy for the staff, which means there are staff absences sometimes because there's a function at their child's school. It's right that they attend and that is why I have such a low staff turnover. Yes, it means we have to cover each other occasionally, which can be a bit of a pain, but it's still the right thing to do. Being involved with my son helps enormously with my work–life balance and, as a head, you're in charge of helping others to balance theirs by setting an example and going home when it's time to be with your family. So again, I don't think this is an insurmountable issue.

Another concern that teachers mention is the fact that, as a head, the buck stops with you. Nobody else at school has that and, if a parent demands to see the head and only the head will do, you've nowhere to go. You can't say, 'No, I don't want to,' and hide behind your chair. You have to deal with it, which can be difficult, especially when you're dealing with a situation that feels unreasonable or you have an irate parent who's not listening to reason. That is when it's time to stop and breathe deeply while you remember that these adults are talking about their most precious possession, their child. For that reason, they can be emotional. Through the training and coaching I've received, I've learned that, by using the silent nod and the odd 'Mmm', you can keep them talking and let them get it off their chest. Once the air clears, you can tackle the real issue.

I'm very straight with our parents. There is a page in the school induction book which explains how I would like them to address a member of staff if their child comes home upset, saying that a member of staff 'doesn't like me' or 'picked on me', or that this or that has happened, and it doesn't start with an accusation. It starts with, we will use my friend Billy again, 'Billy's come home today and he's upset as something has happened. Is there a chance you can give me a call so we can work together and make sure we can support him?' A parent can be unhappy that their child is upset but, if they stopped and thought for a moment, I don't believe they really think that teachers are there to make their child's life more difficult. The job of a teacher is too big for us to do that and remain in the profession. I've now been a head and at the school long enough for the parents to trust me and know that I wouldn't do anything that is detrimental to anyone, unless it was absolutely the right thing to do for the majority. There have been times when that's been the case. If you can start these conversations positively by suggesting that, 'This is an opportunity for us to work together and make things better,' rather than having a blazing row then, generally, parents are on board and want to work with you.

There are also times when you have to swallow hard and take it on the chin. Sometimes a parent will not allow you to speak, so you are completely within your rights to say something like, 'Actually, I'm going to discuss this with you at a different time,' and end it there. It does take some strength and you need to be resilient but, again, I come back to the reality of being a classroom teacher. They are under pressure too and it's from both directions. There is a terrible phrase, 'Shit travels downwards', which you probably shouldn't put in a book, but, if you're a class teacher, it travels in both directions. The teacher is often in the first line of fire of parents' distress and anger and, by the time they've dealt with them and the parents have come to see me, they've calmed down a little because they've said what they wanted to say. In that case, the teacher has taken lot of the flak away from the head, so heads probably don't have to deal with these situations as often as you think they might. Of course it's a challenge, especially when you know you're working in the best interests of their children, but it's a challenge worth overcoming.

Chapter 6

It's a Lonely Life, or Is It?

I've covered what I see as the main hurdles to headship that have emerged through conversations with teachers and my tweet. They were twofold. The first was the loneliness and isolation of the job, and the second was losing one-to-one contact with students, thereby compounding the issue of loneliness.

There is no doubt that, when life is at its toughest and everything seems to be going wrong around you, being a head teacher can be very difficult. For example, I had a day recently when two different sets of parents threatened me with legal action because of my failure to look after their child. These were kneejerk reactions which were fired off by email without them necessarily having the full facts. That is emotionally quite challenging, but that's why you have a good PA who rises above being sworn at! I'm very lucky there.

There are times when the going gets tough and, as head, you shouldn't pass the buck, because it stops with you. The hardest part of this is, when you are confronted with one issue after another, you often don't feel you have anyone to turn to. What many heads underestimate, and certainly I did, was the support and strength you can get from the governors. I'll talk more about this in Chapter 9, but if things are stressful and difficult and you're feeling totally isolated, just speaking to your chair of governors (with whom you, hopefully, have a good relationship) can be very reassuring.

For instance, in summer 2013 our results took a definite hit. It was a 'perfect storm'. We had many young people who were predicted a high D from their target grade in Key Stage 2, which should have led on to their achieving a C. Unfortunately, with all the tinkering around grade boundaries, nobody really knew what a C looked like any more and they only achieved Ds. In English and maths, even though, individually, the results were great, we had too many students who got five A*–C in English *or* maths but not English *and* maths, and that was disappointing. They had all worked as hard as they could, as had we, and it was the first time our results hadn't shown progress and improved, as they had done every year during my headship. This was a first and I really struggled, feeling lonely and fearing that I'd failed my young people.

It was actually our chair of governors who helped me over that difficult period. My leadership team is great but they were feeling just as low as I was, and I didn't want to put my own stress on them as that would have been unfair. I was very honest as I'm a straightforward kind of chap and it was really useful for our chair of governors to sit down and say, 'Look, what's changed between the end of term and these results? What change has there been in the parents' or governors' faith in the job we're doing?' The question was timely, and I really was grateful to Paul Beashel, who handled it so well. He gave me the strength to pick myself up and say, 'OK, it didn't work out and these young people haven't got the results they wanted or expected.' It was a rubbish situation and I felt, rightly, that it was a failure on everybody's part, especially mine, but what do you do? Do you walk away? Do you moan about your lot in life? Or do you roll your sleeves up and get on with it, ready for the next lot of students and make sure it doesn't happen again?

You can lessen the feeling of isolation by selecting a great team to have around you, and I have a fantastic senior leadership team (SLT). As I've mentioned, I was very fortunate that, very early on in my headship, I was able to pick my own, which meant I was surrounded by people who I knew and trusted, who 'got me' and I got them. We know how to work together and everybody in the organisation wants to make it work and, if they don't, they tend to leave quite quickly. The feeling of mutual support and comradeship that comes from people who are working happily together definitely helps to mitigate the loneliness.

There is no doubt that, at times, those negative feelings bubble up. But it only takes one thing to snap me out of those doldrums: the 'climate walk'. It's the quickest fix in the world and it's probably the same for any head. I get off my butt, get out of my office and walk around the school just to see what amazing things are going on with the young people in the organisation I lead. This gives me an amazing lift. Right now, if I walked around Passmores and down my humanities corridor, for example, I'd see kids actively engaged in learning, loving what they're doing, smiling, pleased to see me, thrilled that I want to be part of their education and happy that I drop in during their classes. That walk makes the loneliness vanish. I have a thousand young people who rely on me. How can I be lonely in that situation?

I do understand that, just occasionally, heads shamble about, wringing their hands and worrying about their problems. I'm lucky enough to be in a school where, when I walk around the building or into a classroom, most people are pleased to see me. How many people can say that in their everyday life? Overall, I think that loneliness is a perception rather than anything more concrete. If heads ever feel lonely, then they might do what I do and start walking around and noticing all those young people who, they'll be happy to discover, will be delighted to see them.

Chapter 7

Self-Doubt

Peter F. Drucker said, *'Leadership is not magnetic personality, that can just as well be a glib tongue. It is not 'making friends and influencing people', that is flattery. Leadership is lifting a person's vision to higher sights, the raising of a person's performance to a higher standard, the building of a personality beyond its normal limitations.'*

This brings me neatly on to one of the other replies to my tweet asking teachers about what might deter them from becoming a head. Many of them were very unsure about their ability to handle the job. One teacher took the time to email me and say that they'd always wanted to add some value to their job but weren't sure they could handle it. I emailed them back, and we had a bit of a dialogue and both came to the conclusion that it wasn't such a bad thing to have that self-doubt and to question whether you are up to the job. Even today, and I've been a head for six or seven years, I still ask myself the question, 'Can I do this? Am I the right person? Am I doing a good enough job for the community that I'm supposed to be serving?'

I realise this will come as a surprise to some people who know that, through my work with Independent Thinking and other connections, I've been fortunate enough to talk to large groups, including three thousand school leaders at an NCSL conference. It was a daunting experience, and some will suggest that, because I was able to do that, there can't be anything wrong with my confidence. What they don't know is that, before my annual open evening presentation to prospective parents, I throw up like a lunatic. I'm as sick as a dog through nerves, which is something I've suffered with all my life.

I used to be a good 1,500 metre runner, but I hated it. I was sick before every race because I wasn't part of a team. That memory stays with me. Now, before my end-of-term assembly in front of the whole school, I spend a lot of time organising my talk, trying to make it interesting, entertaining and interactive. I'll pace up and down in my office, running through everything. People who know me well think it's very funny, despite knowing that it's difficult for me. In the lead-up to the open evening, a member of staff will often knock, put their head around the door and, with eyebrows raised, ask, 'Are you all right?' However, I think that embracing self-doubt makes us better leaders because it makes us question ourselves. It makes us look at what we're doing and ask, 'Is this right? Am I certain?' I certainly think it makes us more thorough.

Feeling unsure of your ability is an important part of being a good head. Being uncertain about whether a decision is right and first convincing yourself that it is, before trying to convince anybody else, makes the whole process of leading a school much more effective. Since you often identify the faults and the questions that will be asked along the way, you get an opportunity to hone your decisions and thereby make better ones.

If you haven't got self-doubt or if you walk around thinking, 'I can do this job with my eyes closed,' then that's a problem. If your eyes are closed, you're going to miss a lot of things and, for me, that's unforgivable. Just by stopping, reflecting and questioning myself, I can avoid making decisions that are going to affect people negatively, or improve decisions that have already been made to ensure that they're as good as they can be.

Self-doubt isn't a bad thing. Being unsure of yourself isn't a bad thing. If you need any more convincing that you can do the job, then just look at me. I do it and I'm a very normal human being who fell in love with sport at a very young age. I then decided that the best way to prolong my involvement with sport was to become a PE teacher and to give something back. So, all of a sudden, and more by luck than judgement, I find myself as head of a school, which is something that I have always wanted to be but questioned whether I would get there.

Some senior leaders who worked with me early in my career, and I can think of one or two in particular, would be amazed that I've made it to my goal. Probably they would have seen gaps in my skillset, which they assumed might prevent me from becoming a head, but that's exactly what I became after being the deputy in an improving school. The head disappeared, leaving me at the helm.

I'm always saying to teachers, 'If you ever need convincing, come and visit Passmores.' If you come and have a chat, you'll realise that it's not purely down to your own capabilities. It's also down to your ability to gather the right people around you to hide your weaknesses. I've certainly built a team around me with very complementary skills. They have overlapping abilities and lots of pragmatism, but they also have different skillsets as completer/finishers and are much more thorough than I am.

You must not think you're incapable simply because you're one part of a big leadership jigsaw. As long as you're able to do the things that need to be done, and do them well while leading people in the direction they need to travel, then others around you with better skills than yours can fill any gaps.

Consequently, I believe that questioning yourself and your ability is absolutely no bad thing.

Chapter 8

Change for Change's Sake?

A major difficulty experienced by the teaching profession is the continual change of government targets and to the national curriculum. What is expected of us can be difficult to achieve, especially with the revolving door of the secretary of state's office. For a number of months, I've been telling anybody who'll listen how we can reduce that feeling of doubt about the future and how we should be supporting our young people and our schools. In recent years, we've had a very stable secretary of state in Michael Gove. However, the change in May 2013 from one side of a general election to the other has meant that just about everything schools have worked on has had to be rewritten. That is both heart-breaking and unfair on the teaching staff but, more specifically, on the young people we're trying to prepare for exams, as nobody knows what to expect from future examinations.

My proposal would be for a long-term group or panel of education and teaching professionals to be established to provide strategic direction for education, rather than the secretary of state making all the decisions. I know it would be a bit like turkeys voting for Christmas, and would inevitably involve the education minister giving away some of his or her powers, but that can only be a good thing because over the years they have granted themselves more and more. Placing the strategic direction of education into the hands of a knowledgeable panel that has real decision-making powers would avoid the muddles caused by ministers' poor understanding of education policy and lack of knowledge about the day-to-day running of schools. The Education Select Committee currently acts as an advisory board but, as things stand, a strong secretary of state doesn't have to follow their proposals if he or she so wishes.

Ideally, this panel would comprise experts and experienced cross-party (but non-political) and generally educationally focused people. These could perhaps be proposed by the newly established Royal College of Teaching. The panel could advise on strategy and look towards the future, thereby giving schools an opportunity to plan for the success of their pupils. This would avoid the dramatic impact of cabinet reshuffles and changes in government, and place the direction of education firmly in the hands of education professionals. That is the challenge, but it always comes down to pragmatism in the end. So, what are our options?

We live in a political world. Education is always going to be a political football because it's one of the few things about which we all have an opinion. With the odd exception, we've all been to school, therefore, it's something we're all interested in and have a view on. Unfortunately, as soon as the secretary of state says, 'I'm going to be tough on standards and raise them,' it gives them a free pass to do anything they wish. This means that, sometimes, they might implement policies that aren't necessarily in the best interests of particular groups of students. It is great that governments are constantly raising the bar in order to improve academic standards. We would all agree with that and there wouldn't be a teacher or head who didn't concur. But we need to be sure that we're moving in the right direction. It's essential that we know how children are going to be assessed so that we can ensure they're ready and able to show what they can do and not be tested on what they can't.

The government has to have targets, but how do you decide on *your* school's direction? Someone has to navigate a path through the myriad of government objectives and targets and decide what's important and what's not and that's likely to be you. Heads need to stand up for their young people and give them the support and guidance they need. If teachers don't stand up for them, who will? We need to tackle this problem as a profession. Over time, I believe that strong, dedicated school leaders who have children at the heart of their plans, will influence government strategy. Right now, however, we could certainly do with knowing where the goalposts are so we can at least point the children in the right direction to shoot.

Chapter 9

From Government to Governors

Dealing with governors can sometimes be difficult at times, usually because most people who become heads do so without having had as much contact with governors as they will certainly have to in the future. Looking back at the mistakes I made, and the things that I didn't do as well as I should at the start of the job, I know I didn't handle the governors well. In fact, I fear I was incredibly arrogant, which probably had a lot to do with my being an internal candidate for the job.

I had been working at Passmores for four or five years when I became head teacher and, because it was an internal appointment and the previous head had gone, I'd already been acting head for a while and had been heavily involved in creating the advert for the job because I was doing it and understood what was required. I knew the governors reasonably well but made the mistake of looking at them and thinking, 'What questions could they ask about education or policy, or anything else for that matter, better than I could?' In fact, I got that completely the wrong way round but, for the first few months, I was quite dismissive when they questioned me.

I think I found them a bit of an inconvenience, but it came to a head when the chair of governors, Paul Beashel, came in to see me. He was very blunt, because that is his way and I love him for it. He asked me what I was up to with the governors and why I wasn't interacting well with them. He made the point that I spend all day making sure the staff are in the loop and on board and that everyone is travelling in the same direction and knows where we are heading. Then he asked why, as I worked really hard at that with the students and staff, I wasn't giving the governors the same energy. He was absolutely right.

What I wasn't doing was giving our representatives of this massive army of unpaid volunteers across the country the credit they deserve. David Cameron thinks he invented 'the big society' but big societies have existed in schools for years and they include the governing body. These people, many of whom are parent governors, have given up their time for decades, for no financial reward, to try to improve education. Those governors with children will, of course, have a vested interest and, for them, it's personal which means they're going to commit to the role, and want the best results more than most.

I think that, on the route to headship or in early headship, getting your relationship with the governors right, and understanding that they require certain information in order to ask the crucial questions, is essential. Schools are very data-rich and all the information that governors could possibly want already exists. However, I used to spend far too long prettying up the reports and inserting coloured tables and charts to make them look good, all of which made me resentful. I supposed that presentation was what was important to the governors, but it wasn't helping me to support the children's education. It was just improving my IT skills. So, I took an opportunity to talk to the governors and say, 'Actually, there's another way I can present this information. It's quicker for me and leaves me with more time for other things.' Of course, the governors were delighted. I suspect many of them dreaded the pie charts too.

Heads sometimes need to have a bold conversation with their governors, especially in the early days, and try to find a way to work with them harmoniously as they bring so much value to the school. Governors are the voice of the community and are able to reflect and represent the feelings, atmosphere and impression of the school in and to the local community, whose residents are going to be choosing whether or not to send their children to the school. Also, if the parents have questions about their children, governors are some of the most informed people. It is they who are likely to read the letters or other information sent out to parents. If that correspondence is unclear, then the parents are likely to be unclear. Your governors are an informed set of eyes.

At Passmores, the governors are a barometer of how well we're doing and how we're perceived. It is essential to work in partnership with them and view them as part of the leadership team. As such, it is important to have a leadership team that is not separate from the governors and, for that reason, my SLT meets regularly with the governing body to discuss what its members are doing and the impact it is having, or not having, on the school. They also consider any changes that are planned, which means that not everything has to be targeted at the head. This is great and has definitely bought some capacity for me.

That is what happens now but, back then, I learned from my mistakes quite painfully. I spent the first six months dreading governors' meetings when, all along, the problem wasn't them, it was me. I believe that if the head's relationship with governors is sorted out early, it can offer a new head teacher a great deal of strength and support. Simply by asking the questions to which you need answers, you will get informed and honest feedback and help.

Chapter 10

The Five P's of
Successful Leadership

In order to be a successful head teacher, or a successful school leader of any kind, I think it is worth considering the next few points. I call them the five P's.

Personality

The first P is for personality, and I don't mean this in some sort of hideous David Brent-type way, where the leader imposes their personality on their colleagues for their own self-fulfilment and gratification. Nor am I talking about being some sort of excitable 'Redcoat' character who walks around the school feeling the need to be the centre of attention the whole time. There's been plenty of research on personality and its effect on other people, but the traits that make up a person's personality, sometimes known as 'the big five', can have a huge effect on how you lead and what you do. The five traits are openness, conscientiousness, extraversion, agreeableness and neuroticism. Understanding your personality means understanding where your weaknesses lie and having an insight into what makes you tick as a human being. This means you'll build a team around you that is complementary. It will also help you to identify those times when your personality is not relevant and it's actually a question of removing yourself from the equation.

Can an introvert be a head teacher or a school leader or do you have to be an extrovert? I think, most definitely, yes, a person can be fairly introverted and still be a fantastic head teacher. I know many strong, driven, but quietly spoken and unassuming people who do a fantastic job, so extraversion isn't really a factor. As I mentioned above, it's all down to the team you build to complement your personality. I appreciate that I'm an extrovert in certain situations, but I'm also that typically anxious type of extrovert who, when push comes to shove, doubts their own abilities. That is probably why I suffer from the sickness of nerves before public speaking events.

What is the portrait of a natural leader? If we go back and define it in terms of the five personality traits, the natural leader's personality is resilient, energetic, outgoing, persuasive, visionary, competitive and dedicated to a goal. If, as a leader, you're usually calm (which doesn't describe me), you must also have the ability to show strong emotion. I'm sure that even the most introverted person can become agitated over something that matters to them in their school. After all, you get to know and invest in the young people and their families, who become part of your school family, so it is a perfectly normal reaction. This strikes a good balance for someone who is an introvert but needs to be outgoing and assertive. This is where having a good team comes in, as the introvert can take a back seat and let others lead.

A person who is a natural leader has vision and is able to communicate that vision to others. However, he or she also has to be practical, efficient and have a pragmatic idealism that strives for what maybe is beyond their reach and beyond the reach of the children. You should always aspire, but there comes a time when you've reached and reached and not quite made it, but you've still moved forward and made a small change. You have to be pragmatic. The natural leader needs to be unyielding, very focused on what's happening and not look back when the going gets tough. This also has to be tempered with a good deal of nurturing.

Are you able to be both unyielding and nurturing? I think it comes down to how much teaching matters to you. I'd argue with anybody who says you can find someone who is an effective teacher and successful at working with young people, but who isn't able to nurture or doesn't have empathy.

The job is just too difficult if you don't have these attributes. The natural teacher must have a constant focus on their goals but also needs to be spontaneous, playful and able to see the funny side of a situation. I remember really clearly when Kevin, our previous head, gave me this one piece of advice, 'Victor, gravitas, remember, gravitas,' because he knew it is something I struggle with. It is so important to maintain that separation and distance and I battled with that, certainly early on in my headship.

When I was acting head, many people said that that my personality was so open that I didn't hide anything and showed my emotions very easily. I did want to temper that characteristic but I also had issues with wanting to be who I really am. That conflicted with what gravitas meant to me, so I ignored the advice. I didn't ignore Kevin very often because he was absolutely brilliant but, actually, gravitas wasn't important to me. It was authenticity that mattered. I needed to be true to my beliefs and myself, because I think that is what people buy into. It creates stability, enabling me to operate under pressure and allows others to know how I will react because they know the real me.

How a leader's personality is manifested is very important and every head will make their own choices about how to manage this. Being true to myself and not trying to be somebody I'm not is what is right for me. In my case, I was not trying to be Kevin, or any other head that I've worked with, all of whom have been great. I just wanted to be myself, as that causes me much less stress.

There are plenty of online sites that can help you with personality issues. Probably the best advice is to ask your trusted friends and colleagues to summarise you as a person. If you're brave enough to do that, you'll discover flaws that either you need to be aware of and work on, or you will need to find colleagues who can supplement the traits you lack.

The personality of the leader and their style of leadership is vital to the longevity of the job and your ability to interact effectively with colleagues, parents and the young. Hiding under the cloak of the gravitas that heads are supposed to display means you might miss out on the joy of being a head. Sharing and being honest about yourself is what makes most of us tick.

Passion

In the next section on passion, I'm going to give you a few quotes that I like on the subject because I think they encapsulate it so well.

> *The most powerful weapon on earth is the human soul on fire.*
>
> **Field Marshal Ferdinand Foch**

> *When you set yourself on fire, people love to come and see you burn.*
>
> **John Wesley**

> *One person with passion is better than forty people merely interested.*
>
> **E. M. Forster**

> *Chase your passion, not your pension.*
>
> **Denis Waitley**

> *Without passion, man is a mere latent force and possibility, like the flint which awaits the shock of the iron before it can give forth its spark.*
>
> **Henri-Frédéric Amiel**

> *Every man is proud of what he does well; and no man is proud of what he does not do well. With the former his heart*

is in his work and he would do twice as much of it with less fatigue. The latter performs a little imperfectly, looks at it in disgust, turns from it and imagines himself exceedingly tired. The little he has done comes to nothing for want of finishing.

Abraham Lincoln

These quotes say it all. Passion is such an overused word but I think all great achievements generally start with passion. It is what drives us as leaders, as teachers and as people who work in a profession that can sometimes be difficult. Passion is what motivates us and that enthusiasm can be manifested in different ways, either spiritually, artistically or socially. The passion we have for our jobs gives us the lens on the world that shapes the decisions we make.

I thought about the reasons why I became a teacher more and more on my way to becoming a head. What drove my passion to choose that career? Was it about making a difference? Was making a difference what my passion is about? Was my passion driven by the luck I had and the support I received as a young person?

I think you know if you're passionate about something because you're restless when it isn't finished. When there's something you know you could do better, do you find it hard to sleep or find it nagging away at the back of your mind? That's the drive that accompanies passion. People want to see that you care. From where I am now, if I look back and wonder what drove me to become a teacher in the first place, I see that it came from a passion to give back and a passion for service.

If you ask yourself whether it's the thought of the pay cheque that drives you and makes you passionate about the job, and the answer is yes, then headship and school leadership probably isn't for you. Possibly even teaching isn't for you, because times are tough enough and, if the passion isn't there, where will you find your motivation?

Passionate leadership can shift a school's ethos, as long as people buy into it, and that is the key. The question is, how do we take that drive and passion and use it to inspire people to be motivated and fulfil their potential? If your enthusiasm screams out in every conversation and every interaction you have with a young person, parent or staff member, then people will subscribe to it. They will decide whether it's something they either agree or disagree with. At times this can make life difficult because you will inevitably lose people on the way. However, if you're going to run an organisation that is true to its ethos, sometimes you do need to lose the people who can't commit to your vision.

How does this passion go from being something that people see and feel to something that actually makes a difference? That's the job of the next P for purpose. Without that initial fire in the belly, and without the feeling that 'I'm going to get this done because it needs to be done, I have to get it done, it's for the success of the organisation and the young people in it,' it isn't going to come about.

Purpose

People can be passionate about many different things, which is great, but often that passion can come across as evangelical and can be off-putting to others because they don't feel it in the same way. Tempering that enthusiasm and getting people to understand the driving force behind it, while demonstrating how it can be converted into the good work that needs to be done, comes with purposeful leadership.

Here are some quotes that relate to purpose in leadership.

This is by E. M. Gray:

> *The successful person has a habit of doing things failures don't like to do. They don't like doing them either necessarily. But their disliking is subordinated to the strength of their purpose.*

And this one's by Walter Russell:

> *You have to gather your energy together … conserving it and insulating it from dissipation in every direction other than that of your purpose.*

Here is another good quote from Ralph Waldo Emerson:

> *The purpose of life is not to be happy. It is to be useful, honourable, to be compassionate, to have it make some difference that you have lived and lived well.*

Would that these principles were applied by more people in our society! Right now, bankers and our view of them and trust in them is at a fairly low ebb. I think the root cause of the problem is that we've lost faith in the purpose of the banking industry. It's coming back slowly but, even in difficult times, people still need more in their lives than just chasing the next pound. The popular view of how we got into the current financial crisis is that the bankers' purpose appeared to be about making as much money as possible for themselves, rather than looking after the people they were supposed to serve. This won't be true in every case, but it's certainly the general feeling. If you look at Maslow's hierarchy of needs, it's clear that, once our physical needs have been met, we long for love, belonging, esteem and what he calls 'self-actualisation'. These are the things that count in our lives. I think it's even more important that a leader's purpose is absolutely front, centre and loud when dealing with the organisation they run.

Any purpose-driven organisation, such as a school, has a massive advantage when it comes to getting a community to buy into it. Parents are hungry to know what your purpose is and that purpose has to be more than getting the bottom-line five A*–C passes or the number of students attaining 4B. Yes, parents want good grades, children want it and we, as educators, need it too, but it can't be what drives us. Even when a school is under caution, or you're working in one like ours that has flirted with the floor target (and where we'd still be now but for the grace of a fantastic head of English), we all want more than that. Our parents and communities want to know that the school, and the leader running it, have a deeper underlying reason for doing what they're doing. This sense of purpose is vital.

How do we demonstrate our purpose as leaders? It's essential that we do, if we're going to get people to support us and attract staff who want to work for the organisation through thick and thin. So, we need to be very clear as to the purpose of our leadership, while also making sure it meets the targets and the performance expectations of our students. If, as head teachers, we don't make our purpose clear, and if we're uncertain as to what our purpose even is, then who else is going to be? Are our values part of our purpose? Do we have complete clarity about what we value?

There is a saying that goes, 'If you don't stand for something, you'll fall for anything.' The values that underpin what we do should be the guiding light for the decisions we make and the processes we go through, especially when there's conflict or ambiguity in what is going on around us and, let's be honest, we live in an environment of conflict and ambiguity. The uncertainty is due to the external pressures of government and change, but also because every day is different. As teachers, we turn up at school and don't really know what might happen, so we have to rely on our values to support our life purpose. The fact is that, when you know your values and you use them to direct your leadership, you won't fall for anything else or, at least, not as often.

Leadership is about people and supporting the good of all, but it's also central to leading with purpose, our working life's purpose. What does my life purpose have to do with my leadership? When I'm clear that my life purpose is rooted in supporting the good of all and, not just myself, and I live by that code, people will come with me. It can only be accomplished with their support and, by living and working with them, it doesn't just manifest in you. The purpose of what we're doing allows people to 'board the buses', as the leadership guru, Jim Collins, would say. It allows them to decide that this is something they want to be part of and, if we lead honestly and for the greater good of all, it means that everybody will lead when the time is right for them.

I don't think there is a model or formula for leadership; it's just something that, if you're living in an environment that has a shared and common purpose, others will naturally move forward into a leading role. If that isn't evident and it's all about one person, and that person is you, then other people won't have your purpose and will be unwilling to come forward. Knowing what lights you up as a human being, what lights up the organisation and where the drive is, will mean that people will be happy to put up their hands and say, 'Right now, I share this purpose and I can be the person at the front who's setting the direction, because I'm the right person for the job and because of our shared purpose.'

Perseverance

My next P is perseverance. I'm going to offer some more quotes here because I think they say it so well.

This is from journalist and author George Horace Lorimer:

You've got to get up every morning with determination if you're going to go to bed with satisfaction.

Calvin Coolidge, the thirtieth president of the United States said:

> *Persistence and determination alone are omnipotent. The slogan 'press on' has solved and always will solve the problems of the human race.*

And here are two more:

> *The secret of success is constancy to purpose.*
>
> Benjamin Disraeli

> *Genius is divine perseverance. Genius I cannot claim nor even extra brightness, but perseverance all can have.*
>
> Woodrow Wilson

Those who have heard me talk will know that I show the 'value slide' that we have at Passmores. It's just a series of pictures and one phrase. I have two favourites that are relevant to this P. The first is John Maxwell's, 'There is no success without perseverance,' and the second, which is a very clever picture of a peeled satsuma skin which has been made to look like a person carrying themselves, conveys, 'Sometimes you've just got to pick yourself up and carry on.'

During your life as a teacher, and in the life of a school, there are going to be challenging issues, difficult circumstances and unforeseen problems. I guess they're euphemisms for crises, setbacks and dilemmas. The capacity to persevere, whether it's as a school or as an individual is, in my opinion, one of the key characteristics that sets exceptional leadership apart. Perseverance through difficult times is the key.

It's easy to persevere when things are going well. For example, I had a real honeymoon period at the start of my headship. We had decided to move to a new building, our results were very much on the up, the school was in a good place and Ofsted came in and decided that we were outstanding, even though I thought we were just good. That led to a golden time when we were leading in a period of financial plenty and exam success. The last few years have been more difficult because of changes to examinations, which has meant that we're not getting the results we think we ought to, but we are persevering. That is when the true colours and the true value of any leader show, be they a tutor trying to help and guide their pressurised students in a classroom or a senior leader in an organisation. To meet these challenging situations, the trick is just to keep going.

There are many brilliant ideas out there and lots of excellent things happening, as well as inspired decisions and actions that others are taking, so it's important that we look around us for best practice to ensure that the needs of our staff and students are being met. From my point of view, the absolute core is to make sure that we have the tenacity to keep coming back to what we need to deal with now and today. We must understand that we're not necessarily going to get it right first time. Things are going to change under our feet, so it is essential to be the leader who has that relentless perseverance to do what is right and move the school forward. Perseverance is going to be driven by some of the other P's I've already mentioned, including your purpose and passion for the job as well as your personal vision for the school.

Sometimes you need to find that inspiration and drive within yourself and I believe that the moment you forget that, you're going to find the job really difficult. As I mentioned earlier, I think this is an easy fix that can be achieved just by getting out of your office and walking around the school. If that doesn't make you want to persevere, I don't know what will. Just seeing those young people trying their very hardest, and often needing perseverance themselves in areas of the curriculum or particular subjects they find really difficult, is inspiration enough. As a leader, you've got to have that resolve as well as commitment to the future vision of the school.

Perseverance is called many things, including stamina, focus and dedication, but in reality, it's about having the capacity to do everything we have to and not giving up until it's done. I think this comes from being optimistic about the future and having faith in the next generation, but it also needs to be pragmatic. It's fine to be a blue-sky thinker and believe that everybody can succeed at the highest level. However, it is more realistic to recognise that everybody can achieve his or her *own* highest level. The pragmatic optimism that we need is often intuitive and comes about because, deep down, we can see the path through the woods. In reality, it always comes back to trying one direction and, if that doesn't work, rethinking the route and trying another way. How resourceful are you at finding a new path and taking on new ideas, or looking at new situations and applying your knowledge to them?

I think reiteration is frequently underestimated when we talk about perseverance. Often, you've got to keep repeating and going over the same ground to find the solution to the problem. I know that sounds quite simplistic, but I think that it moves you and the organisation on from purely surviving to being part of a successful journey and evolving through that journey.

There are also the times when that perseverance means you need to stop and reflect on your abilities. Are you the right person to deal with this issue or set the tone? Is there somebody better equipped? You do have to keep getting up and dusting yourself off. I recently put in a sixteen-hour day during which I'd sacrificed home and personal life in order to serve the children. The following day, I came into work to be confronted by parents telling me that I wasn't committed or dedicated enough to the school and not working hard enough! I would never expect anybody to say, 'Vic, that's great, thank you very much,' because I'm not doing it for gratitude. I'm doing it because I want to do it. However, when, after committing all that time to the school, you're told that you don't care enough, it takes quite a lot of strength to get up the next day and do those sixteen hours again. Resilience is definitely something that head teachers need, along with tenacity, perseverance and the ability to be honest and say, 'Actually, we did it. We tried. We did all we could and we got it wrong. The problem hasn't gone away so we have to try harder.'

This could be called courage or strength but it's more than that. It's a combination of those other P's: personality, passion and purpose. When times are at their most challenging and you break it down you might ask, 'What's the one key thing that a good leader does?' Well, the answer is that they persevere and keep going. They get up, they start again and accept the fact that failure is part of a future success.

I keep coming back to the same conclusion. Go and look around the school, take a moment when you're teaching and step back, maybe stand in the corner while the children are doing something and just watch them. Look at the light, look at the new knowledge that is being absorbed, entirely based on your teaching and what you're attempting to achieve. If that doesn't make you want to get up the next day and do it again, then I'm not certain what will.

Pride

The next P is pride. It's for leadership with pride or proud leadership, whichever way you want to look at it.

Let's start with some excellent quotes again. Here are a couple by James C. Hunter, author of *The Servant*:

> *The more I break down my pride and ego, the more joy I have in life.*

> *Serving others breaks you free from the shackles of self and self-absorption that choke out the joy of living.*

Or what about this one by Warren Bennis:

> *Never let your ambition surpass your moral compass.*

Pride is an interesting P because, for those who are spiritual or religious, pride is one of the deadly sins. Actually, I think being proud is an absolutely vital part of being a good leader. I'm not talking about pride in your own self-worth. The warnings about being proud are there because of the danger of focusing on the self rather than others. Some of the dangers of being proud in the wrong way are that you lose the people that are with you because they don't think you're interested in them. They think you're unable to delegate because, if it goes wrong, it's all about you and not about anybody else, so you don't want to let go. For that reason, you run the risk of losing people and their trust in your ability to do the job. They won't support you because they see you as selfish. I don't think pride needs to be selfish. Humble pride is an important attribute for a school leader and, in fact, for any leader. It doesn't just have to be about you. It can be about pride in others.

Humility is one of those difficult issues. In Jim Collins' book, *Good to Great*, he talks about Level 5 leaders and the humility of great people like Mother Teresa. Many of us think that being humble makes you weak or a pushover, but actually it doesn't and I was really fortunate to be in the audience to learn that lesson. I went to see Steve Munby, who was head of NCSL at that time, and spoke to him about servant leadership being about the interests of others, not oneself. I completely agree with that concept and find it very inspirational. However, at the same time, I think you should still have pride in yourself and in what you are trying to achieve, while always remembering that it's about being part of a team.

Instilling pride in an organisation is very important. We have a very clear ethos at Passmores which we call Proud of Passmores (or POP).and it is part of our daily dialogue with the students. Are they wearing their uniform with pride? Are they representing the school with pride? Are they proud of their school and what it is trying to achieve for them? If not, they need to challenge that and change it in order to make it into something they can be proud of. We also encourage them to challenge their fellow students to see if they can promote that sense of pride.

I think that is just as important in leadership. How do we challenge each other to ensure that we have something to be proud of? Let's be honest, pride is always going to manifest itself when children are successful so how can that be a bad thing? It can also be turned around to make the children feel proud of their school and their fellow pupils. Success will follow because they expect a lot of themselves and they've set the bar high. I know some people may disagree, but I think that pride in what you are striving to achieve and, hopefully, will achieve, is something that needs to be embraced. If it's not, it's a tremendous loss to an organisation.

As a leader, just how do we create and nurture that humble pride that attaches to the success of others and not one's own achievements? If I'm honest, I know that over the last couple of years, when life has been most difficult with all the changes in education, there have been times when I've taken things to heart that I know are irrelevant in the bigger picture. This might have been because of my self-pride and concern about how others perceive me or it might be that I haven't looked carefully enough at the cause of a complaint or difficult situation that a parent thinks hasn't been handled correctly. If I look at that situation through the lens of my own self-pride, it becomes personal. However, if I look at the cause of a parental difficulty and remember it's about giving everyone the opportunity to feel proud of what's being achieved, then we're going to have to accept the criticism as well as the praise.

As a head and as a leader, if we can't set an example of that humble pride to our children, then how are they going to develop the ability to consider their own actions and the effect they have on the school? How will they temper their behaviour if they don't want to be proud of something? Some children come from complicated backgrounds that make it difficult for them to nurture those traits, so it is down to us to produce the template.

Humble pride comes with an acceptance that sometimes things have to be done another way, and not necessarily in the way you want it done. If self-pride gets in the way, you're going to be unwilling to adapt your ideas, which means focusing on yourself and not the children or staff. When listening to young people, their parents or the governors, heads take on board what they say, even if it's contrary to what we believe. We can then use that information and new knowledge to create a different path, which ultimately means the whole organisation is going to improve. Then you truly have something to be proud of and can move the school on to a different level.

I'm sure that, as a parent, teacher or business leader, you've sat back and watched something extraordinary happen with your child, the school or an organisation and thought, 'Wow, that's amazing!' I feel it so often just doing a 'climate walk' around the school. Going into a classroom and seeing children achieving something you never thought they'd be able to do is hugely satisfying. I think the biggest case in point for me is at school production time.

I always try to be part of the productions we put on at Passmores. However, whether my involvement is technical or as part of the band, I only ever contribute in a small way. In fact, the biggest contribution I feel I have made has been to hire the right people to inspire the children to perform at such a high level. When I watch our productions or sports events or visit classrooms, I am incredibly impressed with what is being achieved. I'm just a small cog in a large wheel, but I'm part of it, and it gives me real pride to see what everyone is doing. Yes, it's pride, but it's pride in being part of something bigger that is changing the world and improving young people's lives. We should embrace that feeling of pride and strive to feel it again and again, while also instilling in our children real satisfaction in their achievements. As a leader, being able to express your pride with praise is priceless.

Whether you call that proud humility or pride with humility, it is an important part of what makes me feel rewarded for the job I do, and it should not be underestimated.

Hopefully, what's coming through in this chapter is the fact that the head is not isolated and that they are a really important part of a team. They are the part that gives the school direction while occasionally being a passenger or learner. I am including this quote by Ekaterina Walker because it really sums up my thoughts on this subject:

No matter how you look at it, no matter which field you're in, no matter how brilliant your ideas are, success is a team sport.

This is such an important quote for anybody who aspires to being any kind of leader, whether in a school or any other organisation. If you remember that success is a team sport, it makes the prospect less daunting because, no matter how amazing your ideas, the success is not in the brilliant idea but the teamwork that brings it to fruition. This is at the core of good headship, it's a team sport, even though it's your name above the door and you are ultimately responsible. You can only be a success in meeting that responsibility if you all pull together, and that includes the young people, their parents, the community, the governors and the rest of the staff.

Chapter 11

The Path to Headship

I've often been asked to speak to trainee teachers and one of the questions that frequently comes up is, what would be my advice on the best path to headship from being an NQT? My thoughts have changed quite a lot over the last ten or fifteen years. Certainly, as a PE teacher, I was encouraged and offered opportunities to follow the pastoral route, as that was where I had the most skills. I was also seen as someone to whom young people could relate. Unfortunately, I think the days of purely pastoral roles within teaching are well gone.

I took a fairly traditional route into headship, starting as an NQT, then becoming a second in department, head of department, head of faculty, assistant head, deputy head and finally, head. It sounds really simple, doesn't it? In reality, there were many other things I was determined to experience along the way so I volunteered to be a teacher governor in my third year of teaching. For many teachers, the last thing they want to do is go to yet more meetings about school, but this gave me the opportunity to gain a useful insight into other aspects of the job. It didn't help me learn to deal with governors well (as you will have read in Chapter 9), but it certainly made me understand that a head is answerable to them. Apart from what a head is seen to be doing with the staff and pupils on a day-to-day basis, a lot of other work goes on too, which includes working with governors and writing reports. I was also fortunate enough to sit on a panel that dealt with exclusions and, at the time, there were quite a few in that particular school. The knowledge and awareness that the teacher–governor experience gave me was invaluable. I learned a little about governance and finance, and discovered that the head has to obtain the governors' consent to take certain actions.

People either love working with data or roll their eyes in horror. When I was an assistant head, data preparation and target setting were my main responsibilities. It gave me such a good grounding for when I became head, particularly in a couple of areas. First, I learned how to interpret the tables randomly produced and built on by central government and, second, how to manipulate those statistics to demonstrate what was needed. Unfortunately, number-crunching is still a key part of the job . When I became a head and was weighed and measured almost exclusively on school data and criteria, this background gave me a very good understanding of the situation. In fact, I can't see how any head can be successful without being at least comfortable with a working knowledge of data.

Many class teachers are overwhelmed with data and it can become quite an issue. That doesn't need to be the case. Data can be used to give them an insight into how well their students are doing and how well they're doing as a teacher. For me, it's an absolute necessity. I used to be the one preparing the spreadsheets at my school but I now have a fantastic data manager who does the research and produces the data I need. A class teacher has to be on top of the information held by the school on their students, because it can highlight possible issues and help them navigate around problems. So, a good grasp of data is vital on the path to headship.

Beyond that, I think being a good head is about being willing to volunteer. I know this is going to make me sound really old school, but I remember on many occasions just volunteering or putting forward an idea, suggesting I do it and being given the green light. Conversely, there have been times during my own headship when a member of staff has come and asked whether they can do something. For example, they might suggest they run a trip and, before the 'yes' is even out of my mouth, they're asking what they're going to be paid. Now, I'm not an advocate of slavery, nor do I believe in people not being recognised for their work, both financially and with appreciation, as that is the reality of our jobs and lives. However, when I look at the staff who progress, I notice those who make the biggest advances in their career are often the ones who are doing things just because they want to. I feel so strongly about this issue that my final question when I conduct interviews is, 'And what are you going to do for the young people of our school, just because you want to, not because you're getting paid?' The answers can be quite illuminating. If an applicant finds it hard to think about what they might have to offer, it rings an alarm bell for me.

Being willing to roll up your sleeves and offer new opportunities to the pupils, or to volunteer for or run those trips, will get you noticed. When opportunities come up for promotion, you're going to be looked on much more favourably if you're perceived to be more interested in the welfare of the children than yourself. This, for me, is a really big plus, although possibly quite old fashioned. Other people may not necessarily agree but I always did the job because I wanted to be a teacher. The money was great and made it possible to live comfortably, but that isn't what got me out of bed in the morning.

I'm quite fearful for the teaching profession because, as jobs become difficult to find in other areas, some graduates are becoming teachers without the drive they need, just because it's a job. Teaching is challenging at the best of times but, without that passion, it's going to be even more difficult. I wouldn't go so far as to say that it's a calling, but I would say there has to be a passion for teaching. Life can get very demanding around Ofsted inspections or that January/February or end of

November period, when it's dark and grey and the children are kicking off. Remembering why you went into the profession, and keeping focused on that, is going to help drive you forward and keep you going.

For me, it's not rocket science, it's a fairly traditional viewpoint. You have to show you make an impact and a difference to young people's lives. Don't be a Muttley and expect rewards every time you do something. Do it because it's something you're passionate about and want to do. But do get your head around data management and look for opportunities to be involved in the bigger school picture in governance and other school roles. You'll be surprised at how many opportunities there are. Certainly, from my experience, by putting myself out there, the path to headship became quite clear to me.

In Part Two I would like to share with you the school improvement model which I am using at Passmores Academy.

Part two

Chapter 12

The Gordon Ramsay-Style School Improvement Model

You may have heard me talk about the issue of clutter and how much of it I think there is in education, both in our thinking and in the way we approach things. School improvement models and plans are a case in point. There are thousands of books and step-by-step guides on how to improve a school. I use a very simple model and it's one that we've stuck with for a number of years at Passmores. It's based on an educational hero of mine, which may come as a bit of a surprise, because his name is Gordon Ramsay, and specifically in his *Kitchen Nightmares* guise. I'm sure you'll have watched the programme in which Gordon goes into failing restaurants and attempts to turn them around. If you are a regular viewer, you'll know that he does exactly the same thing every week and similar things tend to happen. It's a simple model.

On the first day he goes in and samples the menu. Often, it's quite long, with many choices and different cuisines. Next, he assesses the staff and their strengths and weaknesses. He might sack the head chef and move the young pastry chef into his position, or decide that the person running the front of house should be doing the cooking or vice versa. Then he asks the customers. He goes out into the local community to see what else is on offer and checks out the competition. He then speaks to the locals who don't eat at the restaurant to find out their opinions. Finally, he changes the environment. He might, for example, paint the restaurant white and put in black chairs and furniture to create a brighter, more inviting environment.

It isn't a huge leap from that template to a school improvement model. The menu is obviously the curriculum. Schools suffer in the same way as do restaurants, when the curriculum is muddled, inappropriate or not focused on what's wanted or needed. Moving staff around is often what is required when you have dormant, unutilised talent. It's about recognising the attributes of staff members, making the most of them and using them in the pupils' best interests.

The next stage is always interesting because it's about asking the customers. How many schools actually go out and speak to the parents who *didn't* send their children to their school? That's an opportunity we often miss. Are we speaking to local businesses about what they require from employees and what staffing they will need for the future direction of their company? After all, schools need to provide them with an appropriately skilled workforce.

Obviously, the environment is fundamental. I think secondary schools have much to learn about the classroom environment from their primary colleagues. I feel very fortunate to have worked with children from nursery all the way through to Year 13, as well as being involved in adult training with initial teacher training and university staff. Primary teachers' classroom walls are learning walls. There is so much displayed on them to help reinforce the children's education. When I look around secondary schools, I rarely see this. So often, the most up-to-date classroom displays have been produced when a teacher was off sick or there is an open evening when the pupils have been asked to produce some posters or summary diagrams on recent work. Do we change classroom displays when we change topics? At primaries the answer is probably yes, but this is not usually the case at secondaries. This is something we need to focus on.

The bigger picture of the whole-school environment is about making the place inviting and somewhere young people want to be. It goes without saying that it should be somewhere they feel safe, warm and comfortable. Clearly, it's now harder for schools to find the sort of money that might be required for extensive renovations when there is a lack of capital investment from central government. This is a particular challenge when it comes to some of our aged buildings, but the model Gordon Ramsay uses for his restaurants is very simple and straightforward. He targets the most important issues, however old the building might be.

Chapter 13

The Menu, or Curriculum

The days of schools doing sixteen different GCSEs have probably gone in most schools and this was certainly one of the issues we addressed fairly early on at Passmores. We looked at the number and range of subjects and rationalised them. Certainly in the bad old days of ICT and other vocational subjects being worth 4 GCSEs, we would have students leaving with almost no qualifications. We were putting more and more pressure on them to achieve less and less. That was nonsense and had to stop.

There was a time when we were teaching certain subjects because we had the staff to do it, and not necessarily because the subject was right for the students. We have now moved away from this model. Over recent years, we have increasingly streamlined the subjects on offer; even in this last academic year, we have tried to narrow down the subjects even further.

This has given us the opportunity to increase the number of contact hours we have with students, for example, increasing the time given to option subjects by about twenty-five per cent. This has greatly improved the quality and depth of the learning experience.

One of my big bugbears, and something we tackled in a fairly extreme way when I first became head, was what we called '*EastEnders* learning'. This was where every lesson felt like an episode of the soap in which there would be a recap on the previous episode before the new storyline was introduced, involving some characters in isolation and others not at all. It all finished with the 'duff', as I call it, or third part, where everything is pulled together like magic. I think this probably originated with the practice of having the three-part lesson. When I was deputy, we even had a seven-part lesson for a while, which was necessary for our staff because, then, they weren't structuring their lessons or putting enough time into planning. However, we broke the back of that problem because it was just too restrictive and became quite monotonous for both students and teachers. Those segmented lessons seemed to give off the message that 'this is how we teach', and it was not good.

We moved away from that system in a couple of ways. First, we altered the timings of the days dramatically. Our most complicated schedule was a ten-day, or two-week, timetable in which we had six days where students had five 60-minute lessons. Then we had three days on which they had three 100-minute lessons and one when they had one 300-minute lesson. You'll probably want to reread that!

The 100-minute lesson days were options days for Key Stage 4 pupils, while Key Stage 3 pupils were having 100-minute lessons in core subjects. Lots of schools organise lessons in this way, and do it very successfully, but for us the blend was quite a challenge. I still can't say whether it's right or wrong, and I have to weigh up whether teaching a middle set, bottom set or a Year 8 or 9 maths class for 100 minutes is healthy for anybody. I know that really skilful teachers are able to chunk those lessons well, and more power to them for doing so, but it's certainly something that we found to be a struggle.

The changes did move our teachers' thinking away from that episodic, *EastEnders* way of learning. And the 300-minute lesson day? That was every other Friday. Our system was based on the flexible Friday model outlined in the SSAT *Redesigning Schooling* books. We tried to arrange all the school trips for those days and organised them around blends of subjects. Teachers were often found teaching well outside their comfort zone, which was a good thing, as this helps us to remember that we are teachers first, rather than just teachers of a particular subject. For example, teaching acceleration training as a topic involving both science and PE covers different aspects of the subject. PE looks at sprint starts and science demonstrates how they work. That type of crossover learning was something that we hadn't done enough of previously. We hadn't stretched our more able students to take knowledge to the next stage.

We ran this model of the curriculum for two years and it did its job because it broke down some barriers. It also meant that, at the end of those two years, we had a bank of flexible Friday lessons that we could keep going. We still teach for whole days in some subjects but they're now once a month rather than once a fortnight. They can be really useful, and the value of trips shouldn't be underestimated, but our able, gifted and talented students shouldn't be expected to go out on trips and then have to catch up on missed work. Some don't find this a problem but others find it difficult, so organising trips on days which don't cut across a range of subjects or, more particularly, the same subjects every time, was really successful and worth keeping.

We have reviewed, and continue to review, the situation, in the same way that I'm sure good schools up and down the country constantly assess the relevance of the curriculum to their students. A good curriculum MUST give them a pathway to employment? This is probably more under question now than it has ever been due to current government policies about what should be included. The value of certain vocational subjects is frequently questioned and, of course, the powers that be will trot out the GNVQ or the BTEC in nail craft as a case in point. However, in doing so, they also miss out on the other fantastic vocational qualifications that really do prepare young people for life in a profession. BTECs in the performing arts or media studies can have real value. It's not necessarily about the subject, but how it is delivered and what is accepted as worthwhile in terms of assessment. We constantly review the curriculum and Natalie Christie, my Vice Principal in charge of that area, does it over and over again.

While on the subject of the curriculum, the final thing I want to mention is careers guidance and how vital that has been to us at Passmores. It's so important to get young people to think about life beyond school and what they could achieve, so really good careers advice is essential. When the Connexions service was axed across Essex, we employed two of their advisers as job sharers to offer robust careers guidance and be available to have those conversations at any time with our pupils. They also make sure that the vocational aspects of the curriculum are being met by arranging work experience. Getting the pupils out into the workplace has been an enormous part of our curriculum change, although it is something that no government has ever really got to grips with during my time in teaching. It's almost as though work experience is to be feared because it isn't measureable. However, we've found that the impact on the internal figures resulting from the excellent careers guidance available to our students shouldn't be underestimated.

From a curriculum point of view, we've made big changes. Over the last couple of years, it has become even more challenging because we're on such shifting sands in terms of what is acceptable and what is unacceptable. Nevertheless, we will continue to make positive changes to the curriculum, despite the uncertainty.

Chapter 14

Sacking the Head Chef, or Getting the Right People On the Bus Before Deciding Who's Driving

The Passmores school improvement model can't be entirely attributed to Mr Ramsay. I'm sure many people have read Jim Collins' book, *Good to Great*, in which he writes about getting the right people on the bus before deciding who is going to drive. I think this summarises a lot of the actions we've taken around this issue. Like many schools, we're being forced to look carefully at staffing. It's a crying shame that so many teacher training opportunities at universities have been lost, as it's still the best place to learn.

For a number of years, we've been growing our own teachers. I look at my middle leaders and my senior middle leaders as home-grown. The vast majority of them started with us as NQTs or even trainees and have progressed via that route. I believe schools need teachers who have come up this way and, certainly in our circumstances, we still need them. The rush to change teacher training has been to the huge detriment of education as a whole, particularly in schools like ours. We haven't been able to gain access to the numbers of trainees we need to develop our school because of the relentless focus on particular subjects and the removal of decision-making powers from universities. Much of the input from those outside academic institutions has been damaging to what we are all trying to achieve, which is to have fantastic teachers who can develop fantastic young people. Under the circumstances, we just try to do the best we can.

We have introduced a whole-school coaching model which has helped drive our progress. I guess this may have come from my PE background, as I was very much into coaching for improvement. The first thing I did when I became a head was to approach one of our co-educators/learning support assistants and ask her to be my coach. After she'd picked herself up off the floor, she asked the obvious question, 'What do I know about your job?' Thankfully, the lovely Suzette Mondroit said yes and went off to do some research and attend several courses before she started coaching me. We didn't mention it to anyone else so, when the time came, I could demonstrate that it could be done, regardless of the job you were in or the role you had in school. Within a few weeks,

I was able to invite staff to attend a meeting after school to explore who might be interested in doing some coaching.

The objective behind coaching is to create empowerment and skill people up to make good choices by asking the right questions. There are numerous books out there, for example Jackie Beere and Terri Broughton's *The Perfect Teacher Coach*, but we started off and continue to work with www.coachinginschools.com. The fantastic Annie Boate has helped us to set up a model where every newly appointed or newly promoted member of staff is given a coach to support their progress.

We started a programme of training people to become coaches and Suzette progressed from being my coach to being our coaching development manager and then leading coaching across the whole school, for both staff and students. The results quickly became evident but not in obvious ways. First, the staff started to feel that there was somebody they could talk to and who would support them. Next, I also began to catch bits of conversations in corridors where staff could be overheard supporting young people with their problems. Instead of telling them what to do, we now invest time in coaching them so they can make their own well-thought-out decisions. Sometimes we make the mistake of mentoring young people to within an inch of their lives and then we drag them over the line to make them successful. However, I believe that mentoring is the only way to make sustainable, long-term improvements. It's very encouraging to hear a member of staff talking to a young person about the choices they've made, or asking them how they could have done something differently by repackaging a question to make them think about it more deeply. That is what comes of being a good coach.

Seeing staff listen, rather than pretend to listen, then ask a pertinent question to aid thinking, has had a big impact on the school. This now needs to be looked at again because it's seven years since we started and I think it's time to refresh our ideas. To that end, we've recently invested money in a coaching space. Suzette is working with other schools who are developing a similar model in and around Essex, which has been really good for her and good for us too.

Coaching provides on-going support for staff and students in all sorts of situations, whether it's organising their finances, achieving their goals, sorting out their relationships or getting a job. It's about helping people focus on the important issues in their lives and taking practical steps to look at things differently in order to achieve their objectives. I still have my coaching sessions with Suzette, although I don't have them often enough and I would probably be more efficient if I did. My self-coaching has improved enormously over the years since I first learned to do it. Just thinking about preparing for my coaching and what I need to discuss in the next session often makes me get off my backside and resolve my own problems. So, now, the coaching sessions are more about self-coaching than anything else. Overall, coaching has been a big part of our school's journey.

A very recent change that we've tweeted and blogged about was an idea we stole shamelessly from other schools. The deputy head of Canons High, Keven Bartle (@kevbartle), and I got into a tweeting conversation about the bottom-up approach to developing staff expertise. It resonated with me because, as a head teacher who rarely teaches, I'd felt increasingly awkward when delivering continuing professional development (CPD) on classroom pedagogy. I try very hard to pick up lessons and teach when I can, but I often let students down because of other calls on my time. The further I am from being a day-in, day-out, hour-by-hour class teacher, the lower my credibility so, for me to stand up in front of staff and say 'Try this' or 'Do that' makes it hard for them to take me seriously. They know it's easy for me to say when I only have a handful of lessons to teach each week and they are doing four out of five lessons every day. I quite understand where they are coming from, but I don't want to give people excuses not to try and improve themselves. So, we were looking for a new model. Could the trainer be someone else in SLT at assistant head level? Even that felt too removed from the practicalities and reality of being a full-time classroom teacher.

Speaking to Kev about the development of leaders of pedagogy at his school was like a light bulb going on. We've now adopted his ideas and have five pedagogy leaders developing CPD teaching for our staff and they are transforming the school. We have a pedagogy newsletter and website, www.passmoresfalcon.com. We also have a teaching and learning magazine of which the staff are very proud, particularly if they've received an outstanding judgement in an observation and their picture appears on the cover! The magazine has become important as a place to share ideas and thoughts about books we've read recently. The pedagogy leaders are keeping the art and the skill of teaching alive at Passmores.

As I've said before, walking down a corridor and observing so many different styles of teaching is just brilliant. Just a little note to those naysayers who argue that it isn't true that CPD on classroom pedagogy can improve teaching and that there's no evidence to prove it: I challenge them to stand in front of a class and let professionals make a judgement as to what type of pedagogy is best for that class, that topic and that setting on that day. Belittling any of these factors is not the right way to go, so please get off your high horses. There is more than one way to educate our young people.

Another strategy we've used, which I've mentioned briefly, is to promote internally. We look to recruit inside first, before we look outside. This has enabled me to build a very loyal staff which was certainly invaluable when the school was in transition. At that time, our staff turnover was much too high and the type of students we had required consistency. They needed to know that their teacher was going to be there today and the next day and the day after that before they would buy into you. When I first became head, we promoted almost all of the leadership team internally. Today, if I look at my heads of department and those who have been around for the longest and have had the biggest impact, I see that they are often the teachers who have been on their own learning journey in the school. Sometimes promoting internally can be seen as the coward's way out, but for us it's worked well. Of course, there are times when you need to say, 'Stop, I need some fresh eyes on this' and when my good friend, Mr Drew, moved on to his headship, this was one of those times. I had to ask myself, who is there to appoint internally, or is it time to have a fresh perspective? We recruited from outside the school that time.

The final element to making sure that we've got the right staff is to train and retrain them and, in that way, create a future leader's group. I'm really pleased to see that, around the Essex area, there are five head teachers who have been through Passmores' leadership team in the past. This is absolutely brilliant and it was something I wanted to happen. I want to develop my staff because, if they're loyal to us and stay a while and do good work, they will be ready to move on to the next step whenever they decide the time is right. So, we have our future leaders' group and we have instituted a programme of different training sessions. This was something I heard Geoff Barton talk about at the NCSL conference. I have used quite a lot of Geoff's material and tailored it to our school. It's been great and has offered a very different way of thinking for the staff involved. We're now on to our third cohort.

Many of our previous staff have moved on to jobs as assistant heads, deputy heads and heads, which is exactly what is needed because I hope the vacuum they leave behind will be filled by individuals who have the same drive and aspiration. We talk about legacy a lot at Passmores and the legacy that staff members leave behind really does make a difference. The inheritance of our investment in them and, consequently, their long-term investment of time in the school, has been hugely beneficial for us.

Chapter 15

Asking the Customers, or How Do We Provide for the Community?

Returning to the Gordon Ramsay paradigm, it's interesting to see that he goes out to ask people who don't go to the restaurant why they choose not to eat there. When I first became head at Passmores we had around 180 pupils leaving and 130 joining the school. We were the second school in Harlow to be in trouble on numbers and, therefore, money, as we were down to the low six hundreds. One of the first things I did was to visit our local primary partners and ask them if I could speak to the parents who chose not to send their children to Passmores and ask them why.. The reaction I got from some of my fellow head teachers in the town was to ask me why I thought the parents would even turn up, as they'd already made their choice. Nevertheless, I persevered and asked the schools to organise a meeting and invite the parents to come and talk to me.

How many parents do you reckon turned up? Just about all of them is the answer. What is more, they were more than happy to tell me why they hadn't wanted to send their children to my school, which proved really helpful. Obviously, it was quite difficult to hear their reasons. I'd been at the school for quite some time, though not as head, but I was now discovering what the local community really thought of us. Naturally, these problems included exam results and Ofsted reports. Much as I would like to say that these things don't matter, they obviously do although, strangely, these weren't the first things they mentioned. The parents seemed more focused on the less serious things they knew about the school, such as the community profile. For example, they raised the fact that we weren't represented in the local media and didn't appear often enough in the *Harlow Star*. We tackled that one in a fairly extreme way by going on national TV in *Educating Essex*, but that's probably not something I would advise for everybody. Some simple issues were also highlighted, such as the way our students behaved outside the school gates and the image that projected, which is a problem for most schools. Overall, I learned a lot from that meeting and, just by asking, I got some really good steers and some very simple fixes.

The other major step we've taken is to talk to local businesses. The vast majority of our young people will probably remain at home and find employment in the town once they've finished their education, so we wanted to find out what employers were looking for. We also needed to be aware of what local opportunities were available, so we became members of the fantastic and well-run Harlow Chamber of Commerce. We've since hosted some meetings which have enabled us to talk to local employers and find out what apprenticeships are in the pipeline. On occasion, it's even given us the chance to suggest that they don't bother advertising a job as we have the perfect young person for it! In turn, they have told us what they want us to do to produce the staff they need in the future.

You often hear from some of the more hostile individuals and educational publications that school leavers don't have the required numeracy, literacy or oral skills. This is one of the biggest hurdles we've had to overcome. However, speaking to employers and being able to respond to their concerns has proved to be really useful to them and us. This is an area where parents can play a really important role. I can't tell you how upset I get when I visit one of the primaries we sponsor and see parents collecting their children, grabbing 'Billy' by the hand and semi-dragging him to the car, while still glued to their mobile phone. They don't even stop to ask how their child's day has been or bother to engage with them about what they have learned. So, it doesn't surprise me that so many of our children struggle with communication and literacy later on in life. Often, it's because they've missed out on that vital interaction. Employers do comment on literacy and numeracy problems, so we've tried and continue to try to do as much about it as we can.

The most important customers we serve are the students. I was quite fortunate, early in my headship and just after *Educating Essex* had been broadcast, that Tom Bennett wrote a piece for *The Guardian* on school councils. It made me stop and think about our own school council and consider whether it was just your stereotypical council that discussed nothing but toilets, uniform and homework. Many secondary school councils aren't given the meatier subjects to discuss and often don't have the budget or the teeth to make a difference anyway. So, when I asked our pupils about their experience of schooling, what came through was that they wanted to have more of a say on it.

I invited some of our most vociferous pupils, who were good at expressing how they viewed education, along to a staff meeting. They were asked about their experience of education at Passmores and what we should do more of and less of. The experience gave us a real kick in the pants. They said we were too slow in making changes and appreciating that there are different ways to learn. They were right, we had got into a bit of a rut. We were so desperately focused on pushing students over the arbitrary C/D border that we'd forgotten what education was really about. They also said that we didn't give them the opportunity to embrace new technologies and we certainly weren't comfortable with that. Just by talking to the most important people in the school, those we're supposed to be teaching, we learned a lot. So, food, toilets and uniform need not be discussed at length by school councils. It is much more important for students to look at the education process in the round.

Along with the school council, like many other schools, we formed a parent council. This gives parents a chance to address the subjects they actually want to talk about, as well as issues that affect their children's education. It has proved to be a brilliant forum. Becoming a cooperative academy has given us a structure that enables our stakeholder groups to have a voice and the clout to help us improve things like reports.

We also looked at how we communicated with parents. Schools often don't ask enough questions of the people closest to them because they think that we should know all the answers. Of course, we don't, but many of those answers are available within the community. Our engagement with our community has improved enormously and, as a community person who loves working in Harlow, I've relished the support we've had from amazing local people. Business and community leaders have come in to talk to our pupils about the meaning of community. Having said that, they still get it wrong and drop their litter in Tilbury Mead on the way home. However much I talk to them about social responsibility, they don't always live up to it. Nor did we as children and sometimes we forget that. We won't be deterred though, as it is one of those issues that we will keep going on about. Community, and the importance it has in the lives of young people, is extremely valuable, but so is the importance of the young in the lives of the community.

Chapter 16

Painting It White, or Giving the Students the Environment They Deserve

In Chapter 12, I talked about the classroom environment. I mentioned that Gordon Ramsay generally de-clutters the failing restaurant, making it bright and clean, giving it an atmosphere that customers will appreciate. I also stressed the importance of the classroom environment and how we, as secondary teachers, often need to up our game to match our creative primary colleagues. On top of this there is also the whole-school environment.

Improving the school building can have a huge impact on the curriculum, the students' learning and the ethos of the school generally. Many head teachers were desperate to be part of the Blair government's Building Schools for the Future programme, and Passmores was no exception. The previous Passmores' building was quite dark, with lots of tight staircases and hidden areas. One of the first things the previous head did was to remove a lot of the clutter in the corridors and open them up so students could move about more freely.

Back in 2009, the most remarkable thing happened: we were given the opportunity to design a new building. Following the closure of Brays Grove School, the local authority needed to redistribute the children to other schools in Harlow. It was decided that Passmores would move to the site of the old school and a new building would be erected. Initially, we thought the build would fall under the Building Schools for the Future banner, and therefore would be funded by private finance initiative (PFI). As things worked out, it ended up as a local authority build involving their own money; for which we are forever grateful, for reasons I will explain.

We were very fortunate to be able to work on the design of the new school with the architects from Jestico + Whiles, who were just amazing. The build was designed and driven by people who understand education, the teachers and students, in consultation with architects willing to listen. Ben, Bronwen and Heinz all spent time getting to know us, the school, our dreams for the students and what makes us tick. They listened to what we said and came up with four possible designs for the building. I don't think I've ever been in a situation where people with such diverse opinions were so united in their decision. We all agreed that a circular style of building would work for us and for our ethos. Ultimately, we chose a five-petal flower design, which is perhaps the best way to describe it. I think the architects called it the SPLAT, or the Special Place for Learning and Teaching. I know that we are extremely lucky and those who have visited the new school will be very aware of just how spectacular it is. We ended up with a faculty-based building that suited the school and created an amazing space for modern learning.

Each faculty has its own 'petal' and there is a central space where we meet as a family throughout the day. We pass through it, moving from one lesson to the next, and have an opportunity to say hello. It also gives teachers, and certainly senior teachers like me, a chance to get out and see the pupils walking from lesson to lesson and get a feel for what's going on in the school. The central space, with our hall in the middle and the inclusion centre with the access centre above, provides a real focal point for the school and, now, for the community as a whole. We have almost as many young people in our building at the weekend as we do during the week. An Islamic school uses the building as well as a couple of churches, a Polish school and Kevin Adams and his School of Performing Arts. The community is getting all these fantastic opportunities because the building is such an inspiring place.

Not every school is going to have this chance to renew itself, but what ideas can we take from an inspiring building and replicate in an existing structure? We certainly raised some eyebrows when we told parents about the mixed-gender toilets. People thought it would never work and a handful of parents decided that this was going to be a deal breaker, particularly for their daughters, but it was what our students wanted. When we were designing the building, we included a team of pupils who had input throughout the project. We asked them to rank in order the spaces that we needed to get right, and the one that was mentioned more than any other was the toilets. It showed that we hadn't got them right in the old building and that we probably needed to look for a new model. When I asked what they didn't like about them a few things came up. First, they didn't like the picture of the boy or the girl on the door. Second, they disliked the fact that, once you went beyond the door, there were some things that you could be certain of. For example, you could be certain that there wouldn't be a teacher in there but you couldn't be certain about who else was in there. It could be your best friend or your worst enemy. That made pupils feel vulnerable. To avoid the uncomfortable feeling of younger students sharing facilities with older students, we had year-based toilets in the old Passmores' building. That obviously wasn't enough, either, as they still felt uneasy. The third thing they said, and this came from the girls specifically, was that the cubicle doors didn't reach the floor or ceiling so they always felt exposed, and increasingly so in a world where everybody carries a camera phone. For that reason, the girls tended to hold on and not go to the lavatory, which is not good from a health point of view. The final problem, which was by a head and shoulders the most embarrassing one, was that they smelt. They were absolutely right. I remember walking past the boys' toilets at the old school site and asking the caretakers to throw a mop over them because of the horrible smell, without addressing the fundamental reasons behind the problem.

So we sought a different solution. It included visits to many schools, such as one in Bradford. There I spent much too long hanging around the toilets, which have a similar set-up to ours, although they have a separate urinal next door to the mixed-gender toilets. They had separate cubicles in the round, all with floor-to-ceiling doors and a communal rest space outside. There is a very open entrance so it almost appears to be part of the corridor space. We went with this model although, I have to say, it wasn't my initial choice. It was the architect, Bronwen, who was really pushing us to think differently about the lavatory facilities. I'm so glad she did because it's probably the single most successful thing in the new building. I remember that when the architects came in to make a film of the finished building, they wanted to ask a couple of the students their opinions. I didn't know what the students had said until they showed me the finished film. The then head girl said, 'The best thing about the building is the toilets.' I didn't know whether to jump up and celebrate or cry! The final point on the subject is that we have a cleaners' signing sheet, a bit like those you might find in a service station or restaurant. It's signed off four times a day after they have been cleaned, which is just a little thing, but it shows the pupils that we continue to invest in them and improve their environment.

We are now into the third year in our brand new £23.5 million building and we are still investing in it. We have probably spent over £300,000 in the last twelve months, putting drainage into the field and creating covered areas so people can get outside and stay dry all year round. I remember a time in the first few months after we had moved in, when I stayed late, having been snowed under with work. It must have been about 7 o'clock when I walked out of my office and looked down into the 'heart space' to see a family sitting there having dinner that they'd bought in the canteen. I went down and spoke to them and I asked why they were all there. They told me that their son had a rugby match after school, followed by something in performing arts so, rather than have him rush home and back they had decided to meet up and eat as a family in the school. I remember smiling to myself as I walked away thinking, 'We're getting this right.' To have parents who want to engage and be part of school life, and are happy to use the school in this way, is brilliant.

I get that feeling day after day when, half an hour after the school has closed, there are literally hundreds of young people still in the building, either sitting and having a coffee or hot chocolate in the canteen, which remains open all evening, or taking part in activities. Every day, I stand at the door to say goodbye and talk to pupils who may have had good days or bad days. I now see fewer of them because more and more are staying behind. It's great that we've started offering them activities they want to do and spaces that make them feel comfortable enough to want to stay on after school. Attendance has shot through the roof and now stands at ninety-seven per cent. We've been fortunate in getting our environment right, but there are many things we still need to do which can be done in other classroom settings, including celebrating the successes of the school and its individuals.

Chapter 17

Our Ethos

The final part of our school improvement journey doesn't quite fit into Gordon's model. I guess that is because, whether we call them customers, clients, students or young people, schools are not businesses, even though we should certainly have a business-like approach to them. Getting the ethos right in a school environment has to be one of the most important things we do as head teachers, and that is very much the case at Passmores.

I remember my very first day as an assistant head. I was asked to deliver an INSET by the head on student target setting. It was back in the days when we weren't really given many targets and I recall going through them with the staff and telling them, 'This is the national expectation for a student. You start at 7 points and this is the target we're going to set.' One member of staff put up her hand and said I was being unrealistic because Passmores' students were never going to achieve at that level, as they didn't represent the national average. For that reason, she explained, we shouldn't expect them to perform as well as other students who started from the same point. I was so taken aback at the time that I didn't quite know what to say, apart from, 'No, you're wrong, of course they can. It's often our own expectations of them, and their expectations of themselves, that prevent them from achieving.' That began our journey to get the school ethos right. The aim was to create a sustainable culture of excellence and achievement that would permeate the whole school.

The first thing we did to start that process was to get the sanction system right, because backing the staff was the most important thing we could do. In fact, we got our detention system so nailed down and automated that everything was run centrally. At the end of the day, the tutors would bring certain students to the hall where the detention staff would come and collect them. This ensured that when staff set a sanction, it was completed and students were held to account for their behaviour. This limited the negative impact on their learning and the learning of other pupils. It wasn't rocket science but it did take a huge amount of work. I remember my deputy, Steve Drew, spending hours getting the spreadsheets right so that when a member of staff entered information, it was updated at the end of each day. If a teacher worked in the evening, the updated spreadsheet would make it possible to pick up that pupil the following lunchtime, so they could spend an extra half hour working on top of their detention. We wanted to get this right because it was important that staff felt that when a young person negatively impacted on the learning process, they had a way of giving them a sanction which would, hopefully, change their behaviour in the longer term.

The system of sanctions was very quickly followed by the need to get the rewards system right. As the head of Passmores, I began a campaign that we still run today, Proud of Passmores. The POP ethos remains very much a part of school life. It includes some really simple principles, such as when any young person represents the school or does something worthwhile in the community, their picture is put on display. At any one time, we might have hundreds of pictures of children represented by their house colour and with their achievement next to their name.

We also wanted students to be proud of the uniform they wore. There are pluses and minuses for the wearing of school uniforms and I sit firmly on the fence on this point, but, if we were going to have a uniform, it needed to be right. So, after giving the staff and students a few weeks to get the dress code right and to wear it with pride, we introduced POP cards. This is a uniform card that students have renewed every week. On Monday they receive a blank card with two spaces on it from their tutor. When we started the system, it had five spaces. The card reads: 'Wear your uniform with pride. We are proud of you. Present yourself in the best light possible.' If they don't, there's a sanction and their card is marked. If you can't produce your POP card when asked, that's a detention. If your POP card is full, that's a detention. However, if your POP card is empty, you get a house point for every space on it. Another element of this system is focused rewards with trips at the end of term.

When we introduced POP cards, I immediately had the staffroom cynics saying, 'It'll never work,' and for a week it was a challenge. You would value that challenge, though, when I tell you about a conversation I overheard between two of our likeliest of likely lads. One said, 'I've filled in six POP cards already this week and it's only Thursday.' His friend replied, 'You've earned six hours of detention. Is that really something you're pleased about?' After a short silence he added, 'It's not going away, you know. He's not going to stop until you wear your uniform right, so you might as well just wear it right.' Almost instantly I knew we had control. It also gave us a language we could use that students could understand. Now, if you walk around Passmores and just say, 'POP card, please,' immediately a hand reaches to their top button, tie, shirt or blazer to check what isn't quite right.

Interestingly, as much as the young people moaned about it saying, 'It's all rubbish' or 'You're picking on us,' when they went to other schools they were the first to point out just how scruffy their associates were. That continues to make me smile to this day. So, we got the uniform as right as we could, as quickly as we could, and the POP campaign continues. Furthermore, it sets up young people for the realities of the job market. It's all about them learning to do great things inside and outside the school environment.

We have also introduced a 'positive contact' week for every year group. During this week, the names of the entire year group are put on a list in the staffroom and we try to ensure that someone contacts every person on the list. Staff members sign up to those pupils with whom it's easiest for them to connect, perhaps because they know them or can make positive comments. Towards the end of the week, we make sure that there is someone who can say something positive about those pupils who haven't been allocated, so everyone is covered. There are always positive things to say about young people, however challenging they might be, and the scheme has started to make a huge difference in terms of nurturing and developing independence. In addition, parents who were once loath to pick up the phone now call because it might be a positive conversation rather than a negative one.

I think one of the big turning points for our school was the move to vertical tutor groups, which was driven by Jo Connolly, one of our senior leaders. A vertical tutor group system means grouping students in mixed-age tutor groups. In ours, we have roughly five students each from Years 7 to 11. It is driven by a house system, rather than a year-group system, so we don't have heads of year, only heads and assistant heads of house. Their job is to get the students to be proud of their house and the school. I guess we're as close to Harry Potter, without the broomsticks, as anybody could be with our house points and numerous house competitions. It's not just the standard sports ones either, but dance, drama, poetry and science competitions plus spelling bees. Every subject contributes to house competitions and these even include our own *Ready Steady Cook* and *MasterChef* contests.

Vertical tutor groups allow older students to take responsibility for looking after younger students as peer mentors and learning partners. They have to ensure that the person they're working with is equipped for the day and prepared for success. Passmores is probably seen as very traditional, as we have houses and prefects as well as a head boy and head girl. Many of these elements of school life have been lost over the years, but I'm just trying to increase the sense of pride in young people. I want them to believe that being good is good, and to aspire to the sense of achievement which is gained by wanting to give something back. We care for the whole child, not just their academic side.

I understand it when people say that staff members shouldn't have to be parents to our pupils. Of course, that's true, but we must also ensure that the students are equipped with the skills they need or are given adult help to support themselves. For that reason, we have a full-time school counsellor. We also have numerous learning mentors, some around behaviour and some very specifically around other challenges young people may have. We have tried very hard to improve the links with students' families by ensuring that parents' evenings are not the trial-by-five-minute appointments they can sometimes be.

We have an access centre, which might be called a learning support unit in some schools, which is a one-stop shop for support. It's a circular room with rooms radiating off it. No matter who you are, whether you're an able, gifted and talented student or just someone who needs some emotional support, it's a place that many young people gravitate towards. It's in the centre of the building and at the highest point of the school. The staff who work there, many of whom aren't teachers, are a real inspiration and they work day in, day out with our most vulnerable, challenged and challenging young people. They do it with great pride and aplomb and a willingness to keep going in the face of adversity. Sometimes this includes parental adversity because, often, the young people who are the most vulnerable have the most vulnerable parents too. We also have a nurture room where students can opt to go for their registration, where there is a washing machine and somewhere for them to make food. This has proved invaluable for their self-esteem and well-being. Karen and Janet, the members of staff who run it, are fantastic and care passionately about the young people they serve.

I think the culture of our school is one where students are pleased to see us and we are pleased to see them. It doesn't mean that we're friends or we're going to sit with them under the slide in the town park with a bottle of cider, we're just happy to help them on their way. With luck, they will learn some empathy and some gentler skills too. These will not only help them to get a job, qualifications usually play only a part in this, but also help them to become good citizens, good employees and, hopefully, good employers.

The school's ethos and its development has been central to what we have strived for over the years. We have a long way to go, that's for sure, but embracing the community and our place in it, and trying to demonstrate the impact the pupils have on it too, has certainly been a central part of our school's improvement. Anybody who says that schooling stops at the door couldn't be more wrong.

Chapter 18

Our Vision at Passmores

To summarise the ethos of the school we have a slide that goes out to anyone applying for a job at Passmores. We call it 'Our Beliefs'. It comprises six images, each of which represents one of our values. 'Mission' statements often adorn the walls in school receptions but, by contrast, we use a visual version and it has proved very relevant and makes the points clearly.

You'll have to use your imagination here …

The first image I'd like you to visualise is an air traffic control tower. Air traffic controllers have no room for error. Their entire working day is structured to ensure they never fail. As professionals, they work in teams using the best technology available. Their decisions are checked and double-checked. This represents the excellence we strive to achieve.

The second image is a railway track junction. This represents our determination to get the young people to their final destination, even if it means taking a different route. We need to work out with the pupils and their families what is the best path for them, irrespective of any political decisions that may be outside our control.

The third image is of many hands on top of one another, signifying unity and collaboration. We all need to be heading in the same destination – success.

The fourth image is of some Scrabble tiles spelling out the words 'success' and 'persevere'. We can succeed if we persevere, working our way through the slings and arrows that seek to undermine what we are trying to achieve.

The fifth image represents exclusion. Exclusions don't work. If they did, we would only ever exclude a student once. In our case, it's only ever the final resort and after we've tried everything else possible.

Finally, when things seem to be falling apart and nothing you do seems to be going right, our staff motto is to pick yourself up and carry on. This is depicted by a peeled satsuma skin cleverly shaped to look like a person carrying themselves.

If you are struggling to picture a peeled satsuma skin cleverly shaped to look like person carrying themselves *or* you want to find out more about our school, please visit our website: www.passmoresacademy.com

Vic Goddard, Principal, Passmores Academy, 2014